WRECK!*

CANADA'S WORST RAILWAY ACCIDENTS

D1452270

PUBLIC
LIBRARY
ALMONTE

Salvage operations at Beloeil, 1864. A train went through the open span of the swing bridge. (National Archives of Canada C3285)

(Cover photo) The wreck at Azilda, Ontario, 1906. (National Archives of Canada PA29170)

WRECK!

CANADA'S WORST RAILWAY ACCIDENTS

HUGH A. HALLIDAY

ROBIN BRASS

Toronto

*To Monique, who could well be described
as a word-processing widow.*

Copyright © Hugh A. Halliday 1997

All rights reserved. No part of this publication may be stored in a retrieval
system, translated or reproduced in any form or by any means, photocopying,
electronic or mechanical, without written permission of the publisher.

Published 1997 by Robin Brass Studio
10 Blantyre Avenue, Toronto, Ontario M1N 2R4, Canada
Fax: (416) 698-2120 / e-mail: rbrass@astral.magic.ca

Printed and bound in Canada by AGMV, Cap-Saint-Ignace, Quebec

Canadian Cataloguing in Publication Data

Halliday, Hugh A., 1940–
     Wreck! : Canada's worst railway accidents

Includes index
ISBN 1-896941-04-4

1. Railroad acidents – Canada – History. I. Title
2. Railroad accidnts – Almonte (Ont.)
HE1783.C3H34 1997   363.12'2 0971   C97-931475-5

CONTENTS

INTRODUCTION

Authors generally compose introductions to their works to justify the effort of writing them; readers digest such introductions to seek justification for having bought the volume. In the case of this book it is possible that both sides need special reasons for indulging in the text that follows; one would not wish to admit to having compiled or purchased a book to indulge a sick interest in human suffering.

There are better reasons for studying disasters, a subject that has long fascinated me. Some such events merely happen – there is no way one can predict the earthquake or tornado, and little one can do to defend against the erupting volcano or the raging river in flood other than to live at a great distance from the potential menace.

Accidents may sometimes be attributable to irresistible fate, but more often they are due to human error, which in turn runs the gamut from crass stupidity and callous insensitivity to calculated gambles that failed and thoughtful decisions that turned out to be wrong. The most interesting aspect of disastrous accidents, then, lies in their cause – the tracing of an event from its reversible origins to its final, brutally logical climax.

All accidents are different, and some involve more human error than others. Given ignorance at the time about metal fatigue and casting flaws, the mechanical failures that precipitated derailments at the Desjardins Canal (1857), Shannonville (1872), St. George (1884), Hamilton (1889) and Spanish River (1910) were probably unavoidable. On the other hand, faulty bridge design (a human factor) transformed the Desjardins Canal derailment from a common incident into a shocking tragedy. The Shannonville wreck may also have been hastened by shoddy line maintenance work.

Besides these wrecks one can recite a litany of rail accidents brought about by foolish, even stupid individuals. From the irresponsible conductor who took an ill-lit freight onto the Great Western Railway's main line (1854), and the careless Grand Trunk freight crew that failed to read footnotes in a timetable (1884), to the CNR engineer who seemed to have ignored utterly his written orders (1947), and the inattentive CNR crew that ran through warning and stop signals (1986), the history of Canadian railway disasters is peopled with a sad collection of despatchers, engineers, signal operators, brakemen and track inspectors. Most of them were careful, conscientious employees of long standing who faltered momentarily – and caused great suffering as a result. Many died in the accidents their errors had precipitated.

It is interesting to compare different accidents. There is much in common between Craig's Road (1895) and Hinton (1986), although the former was a rear-end collision and the latter a head-on one. The link between the two is the probability that key personnel asleep in their locomotives caused both crashes. Similarly, the crashes at Murray Hill (1898) and Dugald (1947) bear comparison. In each case a standing or slow-moving train was struck head-on by another train that had ignored cautionary orders and signals. At Sand Point (1904) and Drocourt (1929) crewmen forgot their orders altogether and ran into oncoming trains. Runaway rolling stock linked the New Westminster crash (1909) with that in Albert Canyon (1936). Some disasters, however, were unique – the fire at Komoka (1874), the sabotage-induced derailment at Yamaska (1875) and the low-speed yard collision at Brandon (1916).

Technical aspects aside, disasters often reflect the society in which they occur. One is struck, for example, by the poor railway accommodation given 19th-century immigrants, as dramatically revealed in the 1864 Beloeil calamity. Anglo-Saxon racism was a fact of life for many years. This was shown most graphically in two Vancouver accidents in 1909. The first killed 15 Europeans, whose families received considerable public sympathy and support; the second killed 21 Japanese workmen, whose fate drew little public attention. Following the Brandon accident of 1916, newspapers were at first unable to list the victims' names; most had been Ukrainian immigrants.

In selecting incidents for coverage, it was necessary to define a "major Canadian railway disaster." An arbitrary decision was made that an accident which claimed ten or more lives would qualify for inclusion. The choice was not always easy, as the death toll from some catastrophes was uncertain or exaggerated. A modern book, for example, cites an accident near Medicine Hat, Alberta (July 8, 1908) as having killed 11 persons, but contemporary newspapers put the number at seven.*

The ten-fatality limit ruled out the Mississauga train wreck of 1981. Although it was dramatic and resulted in mass evacuations, the accident caused not a single fatality. The definition of "railway" was treated loosely, chiefly to ensure that certain spectacular but little-known quasi-railroading accidents might be included, notably the 1896 Victoria disaster (which involved a weak bridge and an overloaded tramcar) and the Queenston wreck of 1915 (electric railway). The term "Canadian" was also stretched to embrace the collision of two CPR trains on American soil (Onawa, Maine, 1919).

Railroading and railroad safety have advanced greatly in the 160-odd years since this form of transportation was introduced into Canada. Indeed, even at its most primitive, railroading was a relatively safe means of travel. The worst Canadian rail disaster took no

* *Chronicles of Canada*, printed by Chronicle Publications, Montreal, 1990, page 532.

more than 99 lives, whereas several inland steamboat tragedies and coal mining accidents have claimed far greater numbers.* From 1855 through to 1950, railway disasters might be likened to modern airline crashes; the few spectacular tragedies did not prevent millions from travelling by what could be proven statistically to be the safest form of inter-city transportation.

This is not to say that railroading was a safe occupation. It was, in fact, a dangerous business for employees but not necessarily for passengers. The workplace in general was hazardous, as the *Labour Gazette* (published in Ottawa from 1901 onwards) makes clear. In 1927 (a year of no major catastrophes, as defined in this work), 14 passengers were killed – 6 in collisions, 5 while boarding or disembarking from trains, and 3 struck in stations by trains. On the other hand, 150 railway employees were killed (59 trainmen, 31 trackmen and 60 other trades). Of these, 16 died in collisions, 14 in derailments, 9 in accidents involving couplings, 20 fell off equipment, and 34 were hit by locomotives or runaway cars; other deaths arose from various causes such as electrocution and falling objects. Meanwhile, in 1927, a further 248 people described as "trespassers" were killed (presumably this category included people walking along tracks); a further 34 persons died of "other causes" related to railways (not further described or explained).**

In 1929, the year of the Drocourt collision (7 crewmen and up to 13 passengers killed) a total of 171 railway employees died on the job (43 in collisions and derailments, 73 struck by rolling stock or crushed between cars, 17 falling from trains). Yet, Drocourt aside, only one accident killed four persons (Montreal, March 19, employees run down by a train) and only one killed three (Belleville, Ontario, January 19, derailment following washout). Nevertheless, other occupations were more deadly. It was calculated that in 1929 the most dangerous trades

* On June 26, 1857, ten weeks after the Desjardins Canal wreck claimed 60 lives, the steamboat *Montreal* burned in the St. Lawrence River, killing 253. More than 180 persons perished near London, Ontario, on May 24, 1881, in the capsizing of the steamer *Victoria* in the relatively shallow Thames River. Both disasters were minor compared to the sinking of the *Empress of Ireland* off Rimouski on May 29, 1914, when 1,015 died. The worst coal ming accident in Canada (Hillcrest, Alberta, June 19, 1914) snuffed out 189 lives; 148 workers were killed in a Nanaimo mine explosion on May 3, 1887. Three major coal mine disasters in Springhill, Nova Scotia, occurring in 1891, 1956 and 1958, killed a total of 342 men, a figure that required Canada's seven worst railway wrecks to match between 1854 and 1947.

** *The Labour Gazette*, March 1929.

in Canada were logging (5.45 deaths per 1,000 employed) following by non-ferrous mining (2.52 deaths per 1,000 employed). Construction killed 1.56 workers per 1,000; even water transportation claimed 2.80 per 1,000. By comparison, railway work (at 0.91 fatalities per 1,000 employees) was one of the better high-paying jobs.*

Communications has always been a key element in railway safety. In the early days, before telegraph lines joined stations, trains entered an informational "black hole" once they left a yard, ignorant of hazards ahead or behind. Collisions were avoided by rigid adherence to published timetables, with special caution applied when breakdowns or mishaps resulted in departures from the schedule. The Baptiste Creek disaster of 1854 was related to this "black hole" situation; the gravel train crew on the tracks was oblivious to the fact that a westbound express was coming up several hours late.

The introduction of the telegraph, and later of the telephone, enabled trains to be run in a much more informed environment. News and orders could not only be passed back and forth; they could be confirmed in writing. Unfortunately, there was still room for error – confusing orders issued by despatchers (Wanstead, 1902), orders not correctly transcribed (Canoe River, 1950), orders misread by a crewman (Onawa, 1919) and crucial signal stations unmanned at inopportune times (Almonte, 1942).

By 1860 railways and telegraph lines were generally tied to one another. The next major development in safety was the air brake. Early braking systems had been crude, differing little from those used on stage coaches. An engineer, sensing an emergency, would apply his own brake, then whistle to crewmen to set brakes on component cars. That process ensured a time-lag in brake application; at Beloeil, the only brakeman was not in position to do his duty when the engineer signalled for brakes.

* *The Labour Gazette*, March 1930

George Westinghouse developed the air brake in the late 1860s. Compressed air reservoirs under each car were linked by hoses, with pressure controlled from the locomotive. If the engineer pulled a lever, air escaped from the reservoirs, forcing a piston to apply brakes. This invention enabled an engineer to react instantly, activating a braking system that extended the length of the train. The brakes could also be applied by a crewman (such as a conductor) from anywhere in the train. Moreover, if couplings failed and a train broke apart, those cars disconnected from the locomotive would have their brakes function automatically.

Even the Westinghouse brake was not infallible. At St.Thomas (1887), Azilda (1904) and Queenston (1915), brake failure was blamed, either in whole or in part, for serious crashes. Ordinary hand brakes were insufficient to halt heavily loaded runaway cars in Vancouver (1909) and Albert Canyon (1936). In these latter cases, the cars had no air pressure in their reservoirs and should never have been allowed to escape from their towing engines.

Another advance in railway safety has been the evolution of the "block" system, which ensures that any stretch of single track shall be occupied by only one train at a time. It consists of dividing the line into sections (blocks) with signals at the junction of each block. In the early "manual block" system, dating from the 1860s forward, station personnel and signalmen would allow a train into their block, then turn red signals against all other traffic approaching that block until confirmation had been received that the train with right of way had moved on to the next block. Much depended upon the reliability of personnel who operated the system. Although several American accidents occurred through negligent signals operations, none of the Canadian wrecks studied in this work can be blamed upon mishandling of manual block signals. Indeed, the blame for several collisions can be placed upon train crews who ignored those signals posted against them (St. Thomas in 1887, Craig's Road in 1895, Murray Hill in 1898).

The automatic block signal system, invented in 1872, carried safety even further. It incorporated batteries, wires, signal lights and rails in a complex pattern that required years to perfect. The diagram illustrates how the system works.

A train running in any block activates signals affecting the next neighbouring blocks. Thus, as Train No.1 moves from Block AA to Block BB, Train No.2 encounters yellow cautionary signals as it goes from DD to CC and red stop signals if it tries to enter

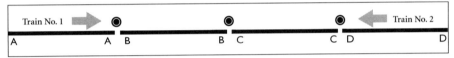

the occupied Block BB. Train No.2 also sets off signals to warn of its presence. Trains passing down the blocks also alter signals in their rear. Thus, as Train No.1 enters Block CC, a following train faces red signals at the junctions of BB and CC, yellow signals at the junction of AA and BB.

Automatic block systems were installed initially in high-traffic areas, notably those close to urban centres, and spread only gradually to remote areas, where telegraphed orders continued to govern most rail traffic. Indeed, absence of automatic block signals was criticised following the Craig's Road and Drocourt accidents. An automatic block signal system would probably have prevented the crashes at Sand Point, Onawa and Dugald. The 1950 collision at Canoe River occurred on one of the last stretches of mountain main-line track unprotected by automatic block systems.

On the other hand, the presence of such systems was no guarantee against human error (Dundas, 1934), much less gross negligence

(Hinton, 1986). It is difficult to build a fool-proof safety system; it is impossible to create one that is idiot-proof.

These observations become all the more apparent when one looks for patterns in Canadian rail wrecks. The disasters presented here constitute a small sample, but some generalizations may be made. They occurred throughout the year, but the winter months had a higher rate (19 disastrous wrecks from November to April, 11 from May to October). More striking, however, is the high incidence of wrecks around Christmas, a time of peak travel with packed trains and difficult scheduling – Dundas (December 25, 1934), Wanstead (December 26, 1902) and Almonte (December 27, 1942). The high death toll in the Victoria bridge collapse (May 26, 1896) was attributable to holiday crowding, although the bridge itself was a catastrophe in waiting.

A few of the disasters were unique – one case of sabotage (Yamaska, 1875), one case of fire aboard a moving training (Komoka, 1874). In three instances rolling stock ran away and could not be braked; two of these ended in collisions (Vancouver, 1909, and Albert Canyon, 1936) while one resulted in a tragic derailment (Queenston, 1915). Nine of the remaining cases studied here involved single-train accidents – one case of a train running off an open swing bridge and eight derailments. Of these latter, three were induced by washouts while three others were complicated by the rolling stock going off a bridge. The Spanish River wreck of 1910 was a particular horror, involving derailment, fire and several cars plunging into an icy river.

The most common factor in these disasters, however, also points to the most fundamental human errors. No fewer than 16 killer crashes involved collisions with other trains, the vast majority being head-on smash-ups. Canada's first major wreck (Baptiste Creek, 1854) was a collision and so was the most recent disaster (Hinton,

1986). However much one might blame climate or technology, the dominant factor has been the people on the spot. That remains true today as one contemplates the Via Rail derailment near Biggar, Saskatchewan, in September 1997.

* * *

Research for this book began in earnest in 1983. Much was gleaned from newspaper accounts of accidents and of the coroner's inquests that followed them. The Baptiste Creek wreck was the object of a Parliamentary investigation, the report of which appeared in 1855 Sessional Papers. Some 131 years later the Hinton disaster provoked a Royal Commission study and report. Other sources included reports by the Board of Transport Commissioners on investigation of accidents in the 1940s and 1950s.

Although no books have previously appeared on Canadian railway disasters, I am indebted to an American author. Robert B. Shaw's *Down Brakes*,* although ostensibly a history of American train wrecks, described several Canadian calamities in detail. Moreover, his book provided valuable information on safety devices, operating procedures and the development of North American railroading. Shaw's scholarly approach and standards were such that I unreservedly recommend his book to any who may wish to pursue this topic further.

A Note on the Maps
For some accidents maps have been provided to help the reader understand who went where. These maps are schematic and not drawn strictly to scale.

* Robert B. Shaw, *Down Brakes: A History of Railway Accidents, Safety Precautions and Operating Practices in the United States*, P.R. Macmillan, London, 1961.

BAPTISTE CREEK, Ontario

The Great Western Railway had a rough stop-and-go birth. In 1834 the Legislature of Upper Canada incorporated the London and Gore Railroad Company. The name was changed in 1845 to the Great Western Rail and Road Company and then, in 1853, to the Great Western Railway. Years were spent in marshalling finances and negotiating with property owners for the right-of-way. Construction did not begin until 1852, but track-laying proceeded quickly thereafter. On November 10, 1853, the line was opened between Hamilton and the Niagara Falls Suspension Bridge. Service between Hamilton and London was inaugurated on December 21, 1853, and on January 27, 1854, the London-to-Windsor section was opened.

It was evident from the outset that the railway had been built in haste. As early as October 17, 1853, the company's chief engineer, John T. Clarke, protested the forthcoming opening of the first section as a "premature movement, and which, if carried out, will be attended with hazard to life and property." Clarke, however, was overruled by Charles J. Brydges, the company's managing director, who was intent on beating out rival American and Canadian firms for east-west rail traffic.

The GWR's line defects were glaringly obvious. Road crossings were unmarked and unguarded, unlike European lines where such crossings had elaborate systems of barriers and watchkeepers. The spring of 1854 softened many sections of roadbed which turned into metre-deep mud holes. There was incomplete fencing to prevent livestock from straying onto the tracks. Engineers confronted with horses and cows ambling along between the rails chose to run them down rather than halt and drive them away. The results were invariably fatal to the animals and sometimes dangerous to the trains. Between December 12, 1853 and July 6, 1854, GWR cars were derailed three times by livestock. Each incident brought human casualties – a fireman killed near Hamilton in the first accident, six passengers killed and 14 injured near London on June 2, 1854, seven passengers killed and 14 injured near Thorold on July 6, 1854.

Inquests on the two accidents in which travellers died revealed disturbing practices and situations. The June crash would have involved no deaths had all the passengers been in regular coaches, but several dozen immigrants had been jammed with their belongings into a baggage car. When it rolled down an embankment, they were crushed under their own heavy trunks. The Thorold accident had involved one coach smashing into another; rescue efforts were hampered by a lack of tools – axes, crowbars, saws, and jackscrews – that would have speeded access to the injured. The same deficiencies of equipment would be evident months later at the Baptiste Creek disaster.

In rushing through construction, contractors had failed to provide sufficient ballasting of the tracks. That meant that there was not enough gravel between and beside the wooden ties. Proper ballasting improved drainage, supported the ties, reduced vibration, and prevented ties and rails from twisting. Without proper ballasting, GWR rolling stock was literally being shaken to pieces on the rough roadbed. Trains had to slow down; published schedules were hopeful expressions of intent rather than realistic statements of running times.

The company undertook to remedy this situation by hiring private contractors to supply ballast. The GWR would provide locomotives, gravel cars and train crews, but the operating costs (including crew salaries) would be paid by the contractors. The people so employed found themselves in a strange position, caught between the railway company on the one hand and the contractors on the other. Some continued to think like railroaders; others functioned as contractors' servants.

At the root of the problem was the fact that the contractors and the railway company had different interests. The former, to make a profit, had to have his gravel trains operating as much as possible. Yet such trains disrupted and endangered regular railway traffic. The situation was aggravated by the absence of telegraph lines; there was no way to communicate train movements, delays and revised orders along the line. The only way a locomotive could announce its coming was by use of the steam whistle; the engines of the period did not carry bells. (A bell could be rung for extended periods when the crew thought there might be a hazard but were uncertain, whereas a whistle would most likely be blown when a clear danger was seen, by when it would often be too late.)

Baptiste Creek, some 15 miles (25 kilometres) west of Chatham, was close to a gravel pit that was being tapped for ballast; a Mr. G.F. Harris was the local contractor. Most gravel trains run from the pit were supervised by conductor D.W. Twitchell, who tended to order trains out early in the morning, even when it was still dark, in his efforts to complete the work before winter. He trusted that through traffic – freights and passenger trains – would be passing fairly close to scheduled times.

At 2:00 p.m. on October 26, 1854, a GWR express left the Niagara River bridge on a westward run. The locomotive was drawing its own fuel tender, a combined express and mail car, a baggage car, two second-class coaches and four first-class coaches. The train was scheduled to pass Baptiste Creek about 10:00 p.m. that night.

The train was beset by one misfortune after another. Near St.

George, north of Brantford, it was caught behind a gravel train; later it was delayed by a slow freight. Soon after departing London the locomotive broke down; another engine was brought to replace the ailing one. Then the westward trip was resumed. By now the passengers were grumbling over the delays and slow pace.

At 5:10 a.m., running seven hours late, the express was rattling along at some 25 miles per hour (40 km/hr), approaching the bridge over Baptiste Creek. It was dark and very foggy; nearby swampland ensured a misty atmosphere in late autumn. Suddenly, engineer Thomas Smith glimpsed an obstruction glistening in the dull glow of his headlamp. There was not even time to whistle, let alone apply brakes. The locomotive blundered into the rear of a fully-loaded 15-car gravel train that had been backing towards the express.

Conductor Twitchell had been standing at the rear of the gravel train, holding a red lantern, when he saw the express locomotive bearing down on him. He jumped before the crash and survived, but a young black helper who had been with him died. One brakeman aboard the gravel train was killed as the cars jammed together and crushed the tender. These were the only casualties aboard the work train; it was in the express that the terrible carnage occurred.

The process probably took less than five seconds. Things might have been better if the express locomotive had remained on the tracks to absorb the impact. Instead, the engine and tender were bowled aside and the gravel trucks crashed through one car after another, pulverizing the express and baggage cars, then carrying on into the second- and first-class coaches. Only the last coach escaped major damage. The roaring screech of tearing metal and snapping wood died away on the heavy, moist air, and then the moaning and screaming began.

The crash had occurred in an almost uninhabited area; the nearest station was 5 miles (8 kilometres) distant. Initial rescue efforts were thus in the hands of dazed passengers and crewmen toiling in darkness without proper tools. Dawn aided the work but also revealed the full extent of the calamity. Men, women and children had been mangled in horrible ways; contemporary newspapers would later describe the carnage in macabre, ghoulish detail.

Fires were lit beside the tracks while the dead and hurt were extricated. Boards laid out in the last two coaches provided some comfort for injured survivors. Pathos, heroism and grim humour mingled with the horror. The Hamilton *Spectator* of November 2 reported:

A young man from the East, whose leg was terribly broken, never uttered a sigh while waiting his turn at rescue and moaned but once when being removed. "Must I lose it?" said he in a subdued voice, as he gazed on the shattered limb, and that was all. An elderly lady of great size, crushed beyond hope of recovery, wished not to be taken into the cars, but calmly awaited her death where she was. "Gentlemen," she said, expostulating mildly, "you will find it very difficult. I weigh two hundred and forty pounds." Her perfect coolness in such an awful moment was not surpassed on the field of Alma, or in the dark of the Arctic.*

The *Lambton Observer and Western Advertiser,* in its issue of November 2, reported the dignified passing of brakeman John Martin. With skull fractures and all four limbs broken, he refused to be removed from the rubble. "Never mind me," he ordered, "help those who are living, for I am done for." His only request was that he be turned on his side, so that he might die more quietly.

At least four hours passed before help arrived and the movement of casualties to Chatham began. Some 47 people had been killed outright or had died on the spot; another passed away en route to

* A reference to recent contemporary events – the Crimean War and the search for the lost Arctic expedition of Sir John Franklin.

Chatham following a hurried leg amputation. At least four of the injured died in hospital. The minimum toll, then, was 52 dead. However, authorities may not have pursued the count too vigorously; many passengers had been German immigrants bound for the United States. Such people were sometimes treated with official indifference; language barriers would have made it hard for them to report casualties; survivors would have sought to continue westwards as quickly as possible rather than linger in so tragic an area.

Investigations of the crash centred upon Twitchell, the gravel train's conductor, and its engineer, John Kettlewell. Why had they allowed the train out at such an early hour? Were they unaware that the express had not yet passed Baptiste Creek when they brought the gravel train onto the main line?

There seem to have been few regulations laid down by the Great Western Railway to avoid such accidents. In March an order had been issued with a few general rules. Gravel trains were not to venture upon the main line within 20 minutes of a scheduled train coming by. If a scheduled express or freight was more than 20 minutes late, guards with flags and lanterns were to be posted 600 yards (550 metres) down the track before the gravel train ventured out, and such guards were to be on duty so long as the gravel train was standing on the line.

These rules were defeated by several factors. One was worry on the part of the contractors that winter weather might curtail their work. Gravel trains had been ordered out at 5:00 a.m. in the summer months; the practice had continued even as the daylight hours shrank. Concerns expressed by some railroaders that the early working hours endangered trains were brushed aside. Indeed, two weeks before the tragedy a gravel train had operated on the main line almost up to the minute that an express was due. When the engineer protested, he was told to mind his own business – that the conductor was the man responsible for the running of the train. The introduction of a new schedule on October 23 may also have confused people as to exactly when trains were due.

The biggest problem at Baptise Creek, however, was that on that particular morning no steps were taken to warn of coming trains. At 4:00 a.m. of the 27th, engineer Kettlewell had asked one Patrick Price, an engine cleaner, if the scheduled express had passed the switch near the gravel pit spur line. Price claimed that he had heard an eastbound express pass about midnight (if so, it would have been a train that was scheduled to go by at 9:00 p.m.). This seems to have been the only inquiry made by anyone about traffic conditions. The next eastbound train was not due until 12:30 p.m.; the next scheduled westbound would not be expected before 8:00 a.m.

Investigations were swift affairs in those days, and legal procedures went almost as quickly. A coroner's inquest was convened at Chatham the day after the accident. Intense cross examination of witnesses by company lawyers marked the proceedings. The coroner's jury withdrew on November 2, but after a day's deliberations they were unable to agree on their report. Most jurors favoured placing blame on conductor Twitchell and on the management of the Great Western Railway. In the absence of consensus, however, the jury was dismissed and a new one, 22 persons in all, was empanelled. This group reported back on the 4th. They recommended that the gravel train's conductor and engineer be charged with manslaughter for having taken their train out in dense fog and for having failed to inform themselves about the passage of express trains. The company was merely censured for not keeping watchmen at switches and crossings. A Grand Jury promptly returned a "true bill" against the two men, who were imprisoned pending trial. The outcome of further proceedings is unknown.*

* Until the 1960s the Grand Jury was common in Canada; cases were reviewed before going to trial to determine whether there was sufficient evidence to prosecute; a "true bill" indicated that a case would go to trial, "no bill" that a case would be dropped. Grand Jury hearings were finally abolished as being unneccessary given that preliminary inquiries performed the same duties. Another task of Grand Juries was inspection of prisons, supplanted in this century by Crown boards and agencies as well as organizations such as the Elizabeth Fry Society. The United States continues to rely on Grand Juries.

DESJARDINS CANAL, Ontario

Canada's first major railway disaster, that at Baptise Creek, had been the result of human error. The next catastrophe could not have been predicted given the technology of the age. It occurred at a high bridge spanning the Desjardins Canal* near Hamilton, Ontario.

The canal itself had been dug in the 1830s to connect Dundas with Burlington Bay in a vain attempt to maintain Dundas as an important shipping port. The venture failed. Hamilton continued to thrive as a lake port while Dundas stagnated; the canal was used only sporadically. Eventually it would be filled in. However, in 1857 it was still in service, spanned by a wooden bridge built in 1853 to carry the Great Western Railway tracks from Toronto to Hamilton.

Two tracks merged at a switch some 130 feet (43 metres) north of the canal. The rails then ran down a gentle slope to a stone abutment, then carried on across the bridge for a distance of 72 feet (23 metres), some 50 feet (16 metres) above the canal itself.

In the afternoon of March 12, 1857, a small train was running from Toronto to Hamilton. It consisted of a 23-ton American-built locomotive named "Oxford," its tender, a baggage car and two first-class coaches. The crew included Alex Burnfield (engineer), George Knight (fireman), Edward Burrett (conductor) and at least five brakemen and express personnel. Some 95 passengers were estimated to be aboard.

It was 4:10 p.m. as the train approached the canal. Switch personnel waved it through with a green flag. David Crombie, one of several railway employees present at the switch, jumped aboard the last coach, intending to ride it into Hamilton. Although suggestions were

* Named for Peter Desjardins (1775-1827), the promotor who was virtually bankrupted by its construction. See his entry in *Dictionary of Canadian Biography*, Volume VI, University of Toronto Press, 1987, pp. 198-200.

The scene at the Desjardins Canal as rescuers hasten to the wreck. (National Archives of Canada C92477)

later raised that the train was going too fast, the ease with which Crosbie mounted the coach – and subsequently jumped off again – indicated that the express was moving at about six miles per hour (10 km/hr), a reasonable rate of passage. It would also mean that some 15 seconds elapsed from the locomotive passing the switch until it entered onto the bridge.

Several witnesses later testified to feeling a distinct shock as the train ran over the switch. This was followed by severe bumping, indicating that something was off the track. A few passengers and crewmen leaped clear before their coaches reached the bridge. Two people claimed to have seen the conductor trying to uncouple the last

coach to save it from disaster – but Edward Burrett denied having done any such thing, and no brakeman claimed similar courage. The story was one of several where recollections differed.

What was evident was that by the time the "Oxford" was on the bridge its front truck wheels, and probably the driving wheels as well, were off the rails, chewing through ties, timbers and bridge flooring. Engineer Burnfield whistled once, apparently for brakes, before the locomotive smashed through the bottom of the bridge and plummeted towards the frozen canal, turning over on its side, then its back before going through the ice into 12 feet (3.75 metres) of water. The tender and coaches followed in the deadly plunge.

A view of the wreck from the other side of the bridge. (National Archives of Canada C121126)

Richard Jessup, a passenger in the last coach, jumped while his car was still on the stonework. He saw the front wheels and forward part of the coach thrusting into the gap, but the rear wheel truck seemed glued to the rails. He later testified:

> The body of the car hung for a moment by the ringbolt which connected it with the truck. Only for a second. I hoped it would remain hanging, for it hung with such tenacity that it was almost stationary before it pounced down.

Survivors told similar stories of jerks, whistles, and coaches crashing downwards. Some kept their seats; others were hurled to the front of the cars. Most victims were probably killed by the impact, but a few drowned as the icy waters rushed in. Edwin Richardson, an off-duty employee who had been sleeping in the baggage car, was awakened by the sensation of falling, then felt the water around him. His immediate reaction was fear that the following car would crush him. A postal clerk was intent on salvaging the mail bags; Richardson shouted at him not to bother, then helped the man out.

Some 59 or 60 persons were killed in this accident, and almost all the survivors emerged with some injuries. Most of the victims were ordinary folk, but one man was a major public figure. Samuel Zimmerman, aged 42, had been a prominent businessman and railway promoter; one of his major projects had been the Great Western Railway itself. He had been very generous both in bribes and in charities – a colourful character with a shady reputation, though not much worse that the politicians, contractors and bankers with whom he dealt.

A coroner's inquest convened in Hamilton and met until April 7. A series of witnesses testified. The jurors examined the damaged bridge, studied a model of the structure, visited a similar bridge over the Welland Canal, and witnessed the raising of the locomotive. While this went on, provincial newspapers sniped at one another. The *Toronto Leader* in particular was highly critical of the Great Western Railway, suggesting negligence in bridge building and maintenance of rolling stock. The Hamilton *Daily Spectator* and *Semi-Weekly Spectator* defended the company in outraged tones; the publishers suggested that hostile theories emanated from the Great Western Railway's commercial rivals, the Grand Trunk and American lines running south of Lake Erie.

Two subjects most occupied the minds of the investigators – the locomotive and the bridge. The sequence of events was generally agreed upon. At or near the switch, the axle of the right front locomotive wheel had fractured; by the time the train had reached the bridge, the forward part of the locomotive had derailed and was bumping along the ties. At that point the main driving wheels probably came off the rails. Engine weight, wheel flanges and vibration simply tore the bridge apart. The locomotive fell straight down, rotating clockwise onto its back before impact. By all accounts, the baggage car and coaches had kept to the rails until they were dragged into the abyss.

The "Oxford" was 18 months old. Between January 20 and March 6 it had been overhauled in the company's Hamilton shops; between then and the 12th it had run 147 miles (238 kilometres). It had been checked in Toronto on the morning of the accident, but as one foreman stated, "The tests we apply to indicate the soundness of axles are the eye and the hammer." These were crude measures to detect metal fatigue; contemporary technology was inadequate to find such flaws. It was clear that the fracture had been abrupt – no rust was found at the break – with the right front wheel falling off at some undetermined point.

The bridge itself was a far more contentious subject. The bolted wooden beams had been strengthened in August 1856. On February 14, 1857, a freight car had derailed on the bridge, causing some minor damage which had been repaired; the marks left by the car confused reconstruction of the March 12 accident as no one could be certain exactly where the "Oxford" had begun to derail. One curious aspect was that the carpenter making repairs after the February accident had been a passenger in the first coach of the ill-fated express – and had survived to testify at the inquest.

A succession of witnesses reported that the bridge had been considered strong enough. No complaints had been raised about it; the worst comments had been that in cold weather it emitted cracking noises. Anthony Sherwood, a civil engineer, declared that ten months earlier he had thought the bridge "slight for the weight it bore," but on closer examination he concluded it could carry three times the normal weight of the trains crossing it. Other engineers echoed these views; the structure could carry up to 500 tons, provided the weight was evenly distributed along its length. Few trains exceeded 125 tons.

In all this testimony one man's dissent stood out. Frederick P. Rubridge of the Department of Public Works claimed that the structure had inherent weak spots and poor materials. He produced samples of wood rot which all other engineers seemed to have overlooked. Rubridge declared that it had been "in an unsound, impaired, and dangerous condition" even before March 12 – virtually a catastrophe-in-waiting. On April 4 he moderated his views, but only slightly, declaring: "I consider the bridge safe, but only barely so, for a train going over on the rails … anything going around would bring about an accident."

In their final report, the inquest jurors could find little fault with the Great Western Railway's technical maintenance; the "Oxford" seemed to have been well handled and no one could have foreseen the fracture that set off the accident. As to the bridge itself, their opinions were a compromise between the unhappy Rubridge and the more optimistic body of his profession. The structure was described as being "of sufficient strength for the conveyance of the traffic of the line safely and securely over the said bridge, provided that the locomotive and cars remained on the railway track, but ... was not built of sufficient strength to sustain an engine and train in case they should run off the track while passing over the said bridge."

In concluding their report, the jurors recommended construction of a "permanent" (i.e., steel) bridge over the canal capable of carrying double tracks – this latter aspect to eliminate the switch which some felt to be a dangerous device so near a crossing. They also called for renewal of a lapsed law – one compelling all trains to come to a dead halt before crossing a bridge. It was a futile recommendation, although for some months afterwards trains proceeding over the Desjardins Canal did stop to allow nervous passengers to cross on foot – something that few bothered to do.

The Desjardins Canal wreck was only slightly worse than the Baptiste Creek disaster in total numbers. In percentages it was far more terrible. Roughly 60 per cent of those aboard the Toronto-Hamilton express had been killed, as opposed to 14 per cent at the earlier catastrophe. Railway wrecks were becoming more common. Worse was to come; Canada's most horrendous railway disaster lay eight years in the future. It, too, would involve a bridge.

BELOEIL, Quebec

When the sailing ship *Necker* docked at Quebec City on June 28, 1864, she was teeming with Czech, Polish and German immigrants, 538 in all. About 80 lacked money to travel further and remained in the city. However, some 458 of the newcomers were ferried to Lévis, on the south shore of the St. Lawrence, and crammed aboard a special Grand Trunk Railway train that was to take them to Montreal. This consisted of its locomotive, tender, two baggage cars and eleven coaches – an extraordinarily large train for the day.*

Most of the coaches were actually windowless grain cars that had been fitted hastily with wooden benches; they did not even have proper lanterns inside. Few comforts were lavished upon immigrant travellers. Such water as they received was delivered to them in buckets. The last car, called the van, was to serve as the principal braking station and crew quarters, but the train was so crowded that even this had been taken over by about two dozen immigrants.

The train left Lévis at 3:40 p.m. and reached Richmond, Canada East, at 9:02 p.m. It was held there for an hour while the locomotive and tender were checked and restocked with fuel. A new crew took over for the second half of the trip. This consisted of four men – William Burney (engineer), Nicholas Flynn (fireman), Thomas Finn (conductor) and Gideon Giroux (brakeman).

Burney was an eight-year employee of the Grand Trunk, having worked his way up from engine cleaner to fireman to engineer. Indeed, he had been an engineer only 11 days, working between Richmond and Acton (Actondale); he was unfamiliar with the route from

* Newspaper reports and railway personnel disagreed on the composition of the train; another version had it composed of four baggage cars, six "boxcars," a second-class coach and the brake van.

Acton to Montreal. Accordingly, he inquired as to whether another man might take this train, only to be told that no one else was available.

Facing a night run over strange tracks, and worried about his inexperience, Burney asked his brakeman to join him in the cab, even though this meant that Giroux had to leave his regular post. Conductor Finn took over the brake van. However, Giroux returned to his braking station when the train halted to refuel at St. Hilaire at 1:05 a.m. on the morning of June 29. The crew spent a few minutes throwing wood aboard the tender.

From St. Hilaire the line turned south on a descending grade, running parallel to the Richelieu River before rounding a curve to the right and entering upon a bridge that spanned the Richelieu. On the other side was Beloeil Station, which would lend its name to the impending disaster. The heart of the tragedy lay in that bridge.

River traffic along the Richelieu was frequent, and the 50-foot (15-metre) clearance between bridge and water was insufficient for steamers and towed sailing craft. Consequently, a portion of the bridge on the Beloeil side swung open to permit boats to pass; this action was controlled by a bridgemaster. Orders were that rail traffic had precedence over boats, so vessels were to be halted 15 minutes before the arrival of a scheduled train. However, bridgemaster Nicholas Griffin was unaware of the special immigrant train that was approaching. He routinely opened the span for a southbound steam tug, the *Champlain*, pulling a string of eight barges and sailing vessels.

Rule 24 in the Grand Trunk's book of instructions required all locomotives approaching the swing bridge to halt short of the structure so that crews might confirm the span was closed. Only then were they to proceed. In practice, rules of this nature were routinely ignored by trainmen and violations went unreported by bridgemasters. It was considered sufficient that trains slow down as they ventured upon the bridge; the modern equivalent would be motorists who slow to a crawl but do not fully halt at a "Stop" sign.

The bridge did have some safety equipment. A semaphore signal was located on the Beloeil side of the bridge, but it was difficult to see from westbound trains and was of only marginal use at night. It would certainly not be obvious to any rail crew that was not conscientiously looking for it in the darkness. A set of red lanterns on the swing bridge was displayed down the tracks when the span was open.

At about 1:15 a.m. the immigrant special chugged out of St. Hilaire, gathering speed as it descended the grade. A row of trees on the right screened engineer Burney's view of the river and bridge. As the locomotive rounded the curve and began its run across the bridge, the engineer discerned the dull red glow of warning lanterns. He knew he was going too fast; the combined forces of gravity and momentum, operating through the sloping grade and the heavy string of coaches pushing from behind, were forcing the locomotive forward at about 12-15 miles per hour (20-25 km/hr). He began whistling for brakes. There was no response. Giroux, the brakeman, was preoccupied with trimming a lamp and first had to put it down before reacting. By then time had run out; the locomotive plunged into the open draw, pulling every coach after it.

The engine itself struck a grain-laden barge and bounced into the water; miraculously, its engineer would survive the disaster. The cars, however, piled up on one another in an extended crash – a cacophony lasting at least 15 seconds. Victims were trapped in the wreckage and in the water. Coaches broke open, scattering their occupants.

First on the scene to help were the men who had been aboard the steam tug and barges. They had witnessed the train's approach and

fatal plunge, and one or two had narrowly escaped being caught under debris. Rural French Canada was well serviced by medical doctors; these and volunteers from villages around quickly converged on the site. However, their work was impeded by the language barrier that stood between immigrants and those attempting to help them. When word of the wreck reached Montreal, a relief train was despatched, carrying several representatives of that city's German and Polish communities to assist as interpreters.

Burney had emerged with nothing worse than bruises; his fireman was killed, along with conductor Finn and 97 passengers. The Beloeil bridge disaster was thus the most terrible wreck in Canadian railway history.

Such a calamity was followed by many events that would puzzle if not shock Canadians today. The immediate handling of survivors was a case in point. In spite of language difficulties, these were accorded generous hospitality by villagers and country folk until the Grand Trunk conveyed the unfortunate newcomers to Montreal. Negotiations for compensation began at once, with the local German Society acting on behalf of the victims. On July 5, only one week after the wreck, the *Montreal Gazette* announced what terms had been reached. The Grand Trunk Railway would pay from $5 to $20 per passenger for personal injuries; those who had lost members of their family would receive between $25 and $1,200 depending on the estimated earning power of the deceased kin. The German Society, although accepting these figures, complained that the company was paying niggardly compensation for baggage losses. The Grand Trunk, for its part, disowned the actions of one of its Montreal clerks who asked survivors to sign waiver-of-claim forms they could not read, then tried to hustle them out of the city by the next train.

The coroner's inquest convened on June 29, the day of the acci-

(Facing page) A jumbled pile of rolling stock beneath the open span at Beloeil. (National Archives of Canada C3286)

dent, raised many eyebrows at the time and would greatly offend modern standards of fair play. From the outset, William Burney, as the engineer who had run his train into the river and been fool enough to survive, stood as the accused. He was not permitted to testify on his own behalf, and a lawyer named Devlin was denied permission to represent Burney. (Devlin, obviously a burr to the Grand Trunk Railway, subsequently acted on behalf of surviving immigrants in seeking compensation.) A mildly critical report in the *Montreal Daily Witness* outraged one juror, who claimed that the panel had been accused of being under the influence of the railway company.

Certainly there was an evident imbalance of forces. Burney could question witnesses but was otherwise nearly defenceless; the Grand Trunk meanwhile marshalled a strong contingent of managers and lawyers to defend the corporate position. The most perceptive and probing questions evidently came from the jurors themselves.

The inquest heard conflicting evidence. Thomas King, the locomotive foreman in Richmond and the man who had assigned Burney to the train, denied that the unfortunate engineer had asked not to be given that task. On the other hand, brakeman Giroux testified about being in the cab from Richmond to St. Hilaire, during which time he had to identify many upcoming stops and stations for Burney, indicating the engineer's unfamiliarity with the route.

How ignorant was Burney of the tracks and signals that lay between Richmond and Montreal? Several of his colleagues were called to the stand. Although he had been an engineer only 11 days and had not made the Richmond-Montreal run in that period, he had been a fireman for several years. In that capacity he might have crossed the Beloeil bridge as many as 30 times, either with express trains or freights. Since firemen were regarded as engineers-in-waiting, shar-

An engraving of the Beloeil wreck shows the boat on which the train fell. (National Archives of Canada PA138680)

ing lookout duties with engineers, it was suggested that Burney should have been aware of all rules and hazards along the line.

The inquest jury concluded its sittings on July 12, 1864. It spread blame for the disaster. Although William Burney was accused of "gross negligence," Thomas King was also scolded. The jury stated: "The locomotive foreman at Richmond displayed a want of judgement and caution in putting a driver in charge of a train without previously ascertaining by personal investigation whether such driver knew the road and signals."

Having singled out these two men for censure, the jury went on to condemn the frequent breaches of Rule 24, which had so often been ignored with violations unreported by bridgemasters and other employees. They stated that a minimum of two brakemen were needed on such long, heavy trains. Finally, they suggested that the Beloeil bridge be rebuilt to eliminate the swing section, although that would not be practical so long as masted river traffic passed that section of the Richelieu.

Press reaction to the inquest was mixed. The *Gazette* carried a lengthy editorial on July 14 in which it criticized other papers for their comments, particularly the *Montreal Daily Witness* for being sceptical of Grand Trunk evidence and the Toronto *Globe* for attacking the practice of using freight cars to transport immigrants. On this latter point the *Gazette* grudgingly conceded that such actions were "unfortunate" but not "criminal" and thus excused the company. King and Burney were deemed more culpable in the eyes of the *Gazette*'s editor; the engineer, declared the newspaper, was not only ignorant of the line but knew he was ignorant and thus was under a special obligation to be careful. The paper also condemned any signs of public sympathy that might be rallied in Burney's favour.

William Burney was not prosecuted – an indication that railway officials either accepted some blame or deemed it unwise to have the accident aired in court where a lawyer might assist the accused. The engineer was dismissed from Grand Trunk service. One amateur historian has stated that he remained in Montreal, "broken mentally and physically," scorned and taunted by children and adults as the culprit in the Beloeil bridge disaster.*

* Omer S.A. Lavallée, *Beloeil*, Canadian Railroad Historical Association, Montreal, 1965.

SHANNONVILLE, Ontario

"Railroads are my politics" – so proclaimed Sir Allan Napier McNab, a leading Canadian entrepreneur and statesman of the 1840s and 1850s. Railways were important matters to many 19th-century politicians, and almost every facet of line construction and management was subject to partisan interpretation. This was demonstrated in the investigations that followed the wreck of a Grand Trunk express in the early hours of June 22, 1872.

The train was eastbound from Toronto to Montreal with a full load of passengers. Strung out behind the engine and tender were a combined baggage and express car, a smoking (lounge) car, a second-class coach, two first-class coaches and a sleeping car. The first-class cars were occupied chiefly by Anglican clergymen who had been attending a synod in Toronto. A party of lumbermen bound for Quebec made up most of the estimated 55 travellers in the second-class coach.

On this particular night the train was running about 20 minutes late. The crew had managed to make up about five minutes on the run to Belleville, but that time had been lost in the process of taking on more wood for the locomotive. The train pulled out again at about 20 minutes past midnight, chugging along a straight piece of line that rose and fell gently as it skirted the north shore of Lake Ontario. The train slowed as it passed through the village of Shannonville, then began gathering speed as it crossed the Salmon River, a minor stream that was spanned by an 8-foot (2.5-metre) embankment rather than a bridge.

Several passengers later claimed that the express was swaying markedly and that one could scarcely stand in the coaches. To some this meant that the roadbed was too rough; others would conclude that the train was going too quickly; still others saw nothing unusual in the rocking motion which was common enough to rail travellers into this century. Conductor Henry Nielson, walking from the rear coach forward, paused and sat down in a first-class coach to answer a question put to him by a passenger. That brief delay probably saved his life.

At approximately 1:00 a.m. the front truck of the locomotive derailed. The engine began thumping along the ties. Engineer John Hibbert whistled for brakes, then tried to reverse his mount. Things happened too fast. Abruptly the locomotive fell over the embankment and came to rest on its side. The baggage car shot past the engine/tender combination. Men working in it were thrown about and shaken up but emerged unhurt. Those in the following smoker and second-class coach were far less fortunate.

These two cars telescoped each other, with half of one rammed into its companion. Even then, fatalities might have been minimal had not the cars landed on top of the engine, shearing away a safety valve and dome. Instantly a tornado of scalding steam exploded among the passengers. Flesh was cooked; people drawing a breath to scream sucked the deadly vapour into their lungs. It probably took only a half-minute for the boiler to release its steam under pressure, but that was all the time needed to render this Canada's sixth most deadly rail crash.

The two first-class coaches had derailed but remained upright; the sleeping car was still on the tracks. Passengers and crewmen converged on the wrecked coaches, with conductor Nielson and a travelling businessman, Robert Roddy, leading rescue efforts using crowbars (their availability showed that some lessons had been learned from Baptiste Creek and Desjardins Canal). A brakeman, John Rundle, lit a red lantern and arranged for any following trains to be flagged down. A telegram from Shannonville summoned a special train from Belleville with ten doctors. Until that arrived, the sleeping car served as a first-aid station. The dead were laid out by the tracks; the scalded survivors found the cool night air added to their agony.

Two men including engineer Hibbert had been killed outright by the impact. Some 65 people had been scalded terribly, and six of these succumbed at the crash site. A freight shed at the Belleville station, initially serving as a burn hospital, witnessed more deaths. By July 2 the toll had reached 34.

A doctor named Burdett (not further identified in the newspaper accounts) had been among the first of the physicians on the scene. He quickly convened a coroner's inquest which went over the ground on the 22nd, heard witnesses on the 24th, and promptly brought in a conclusion. Although two people had described the track as being less than satisfactory, the jury declared that the wreck had been "purely accidental," with the track "in good condition," and the engineer "a sober, efficient and careful officer." The derailment had been caused by a flange breaking on a right-hand wheel on the locomotive's front truck. The verdict concluded with glowing words for the co-operation extended to the inquest by Grand Trunk employees.

Even by the standards of the day, it had been a perfunctory affair. The Toronto *Daily Globe* described the investigation as a "farce," branded most of the witnesses as Grand Trunk employees, sniped at a local civil engineer who had testified as probably being associated with the company, and demanded another inquest. Ontario's Liberal government agreed; on June 25 – the same day as the *Globe* came out swinging – Attorney General Adam Crooks appointed coroner Charles Graeme to hold a second inquiry.

The decision to convene a second inquest set newspapers bickering. The Toronto *Mail* (Conservative) and *Daily Globe* (Liberal) were especially partisan; they seldom referred to one another by name, preferring to attack "the Grit organ" and "the Tory organ." The *Mail* opened the feud over the wreck inquiry with an article on the 26th describing the *Globe*'s hostile editorial as "scandalous ... universally condemned ... glaringly false." The *Mail* declared that William Ferguson, the civil engineer deemed suspect by the *Globe*, was quite neutral. The *Mail* returned to the subject on the 27th with a lengthy editorial – two full columns of fine type – that defended the original inquest, attacked the *Globe* for demanding impossible amounts of "scientific evidence," and concluded: "The Ontario government, it appears, has ordered a new investigation, thus lending itself as it can to the unworthy objects which actuate its principal newspaper supporter. What new facts it can obtain we are at a loss to imagine."

George Brown's *Daily Globe*, for its part, retaliated with heavy-handed sarcasm:

> It is far less important that thirty or forty men, women and children should die a most horrible death, or that as many more should be writhing in the most excruciating agonies, some of them, if they survive, certain to bear the consequences of their injuries for the rest of their lives, than that a Grand Trunk engine inspector should be found to have failed to do his duty, or a Grand Trunk engine driver to have run his train at too high a rate of speed, or a piece of Grand Trunk track to have been out of order.

The *Globe*'s hostility was related to more than the haste with which the first inquiry had been conducted. It was Liberal dogma that the Grand Trunk Railway was a corrupt enterprise with close links to Sir John A. Macdonald's Conservatives. The company's general manager, Charles Brydges (formerly of the Great Western Railway), was indeed friendly with the Tory prime minister, but his knowledge of railroading was so thorough that even Liberal ministries would eventually swallow their reservations and employ him.* For the moment, however, the *Globe* was incensed with an inquest that had not only proceeded in haste but had concluded by heaping praise on the hated corporation.

The second inquiry was much more searching than the first; a broader raange of witnesses was called; cross-examination was more comprehensive. All the same, most of the earlier jury's conclusions were confirmed. Witnesses agreed at both sets of hearings that engineer Hibbert had been experienced, skilled and responsible, not likely to take chances in pursuit of making up lost time.

The speed of the train was discussed at length. Most witnesses were adamant that the express had slowed for the Shannonville station and had only begun to gather speed once more when the accident occurred. A pace of about 25 miles per hour (38 km/hr) seemed the most likely rate.

That a three-inch chunk of metal had come off a wheel flange was undisputed – but had the break come before or after the derailment? Could the danger have been detected earlier? It seemed that the wheel had been intact immediately before the fracture; there was no sign of an earlier crack or flaw; a wheel check in Belleville (an inspector tapping wheels with a hammer) had given no hint of an existing fault.

Three civil engineers – Francis Shanly, John Henry Dumble and Thomas Keefer – testified at the second inquest. They agreed that the roadbed had not been particularly good, but each differed from the others with respect to details. Keefer felt the tracks had been poorly ballasted; the others concluded that ballasting had been adequate.

* See the entry on Brydges in *Dictionary of Canadian Biography*, Volume XI, University of Toronto Press, 1982, pp. 121-125.

Dumble, however, brought forward some disturbing observations. Having gone over the tracks for some 600 yards (180 metres) he reported that the rails had been poorly spiked. In some places the fishplates that held rails to ties were secured with only one spike, and some spikes had been driven only part-way into the ties. Such ill-secured rails might have exaggerated the rocking motion of the train, which in turn might have strained the wheel flange to the breaking point.

On the other hand, there was no proof that the roadbed had created any more swaying than one normally encountered on contemporary trains, and it could not be stated categorically that the motion of the engine had so buffeted its wheel on the rails that the flange had fractured. The fact that a rescue train had passed safely over the questionable track section only an hour after the accident suggested that the roadbed was safe enough; however, the rescue train had been proceeding very slowly. Everything was inconclusive.

While the inquest was going forward the *Mail* and *Globe* reported proceedings in their own unique ways. The *Globe* printed every critical statement brought out about the line; it devoted exceptional space to evidence of the three civil engineers, particularly Dumble. The *Mail*, on the other hand, seemed intent on minimizing the coverage of engineering critiques.

On July 12 the second inquest brought in its findings, agreed upon by 13 of 18 jurors. Their report confirmed the earlier body's conclusions – that the derailment had been caused by a locomotive wheel breaking. In this case they held back from declaring the Grand Trunk personnel to be blameless, but they did admit to being unable to determine the cause of the fracture; the evidence heard had been too contradictory to allow definitive statements.

It was to be expected that the Toronto *Daily Globe* would not find this verdict to be completely satisfactory. The paper grumbled editorially about speeding trains and unsafe tracks, but it grudgingly admitted that the second inquest had been thorough and non-partisan. The *Mail*, for its part, exulted in what it perceived to be the humiliation of the *Globe*:

Taking advantage of a holocaust which, from no cause that could have been foreseen or provided against, fell to the unfortunate lot of the Grand Trunk Railway, the Grit organ in this city, true to its mortal antagonism to that road, employed every engine in its power to force a jury to hold Mr. Brydges and his colleagues responsible. In its fiendish attack on the Grand Trunk, the organ received the assistance of the Ontario government. The plot has disastrously failed. The second jury has substantiated the verdict of the first and declared that the cause of the accident remains a mystery.... The five jurors who refused to sign the verdict are Grits.... Once more Grit malignity and Grit bitterness of feeling towards the Grand Trunk have come to naught, even though the power of the local Government was brought to bear in their behalf.

The Toronto papers had done their best to turn a human tragedy into a political dogfight; both journals cheapened the disaster by using it as cannon fodder in their partisan battle. Coverage of the Shannonville inquests speaks volumes about newspaper standards of the day.

KOMOKA, Ontario

Some of the railroading practices on Canadian trains in the 19th century were peculiar; others were downright dangerous. Both facets came together on a Great Western Railway train run out of London on the evening of February 28, 1874.

A frequently-used device then was the "accommodation train," made up by stringing together cars and coaches differing greatly in function and manufacture. In western Ontario, the most common type of mixed train involved several oil tank cars travelling with a baggage car and one or two coaches. Such trains shuttled around the area, which was then a major petroleum-producing region with wells near Petrolia and Wyoming; refining facilities were centred upon London.

Federal law backed up by railway company rules stipulated that on passenger trains there should be a device to allow conductors to transmit emergency signals to engineers. That meant running a bell rope the length of the train. On freights and "accommodation trains" this proved to be a troublesome matter. Train crews complained that the ropes snagged or broke on tanker cars, sometimes whipping under the trains and fouling the axles. A brakeman had fallen under a moving train and lost both legs while trying to free a tangled bell cord. The Great Western Railway formally recognized the problem in 1870 when it published a regulation permitting crews of long freights to dispense with bell cords. However, such devices continued to be mandatory on passenger trains.

Accommodation trains were neither pure freights nor pure expresses. Crews adopted the procedure of disconnecting bell cords while tank cars were in the train, reconnecting the signal to the engine once the tankers had been dropped off. No company official approved the measure, but station masters were aware that it was being done. It would seem that knowledge of the problem and its risky solution did not extend any higher in the chain of command; simply stated, nobody bothered to report the situation to middle and senior management.

The train which dramatized the problem was composed of an engine and tender, three oil tankers, a baggage car, a second-class smoker and a first-class coach. It departed from London for Sarnia at 6:28 p.m. Aboard were about 60 passengers, most of them sitting in the rear coach. The train chugged up a long grade, then began a descent towards Komoka Station (now a London suburb). Estimates of the speed varied widely, from 25 to 40 miles per hour (40-60 km/hr). The most likely pace seems to have been about 25 miles per hour (40 km/hr), judging from the numbers of people who survived with injuries after jumping.

Trains were lit with coal oil lamps that were secured to walls with a spring-clamp. One such lamp was in the "saloon" or "water closet" (in modern language, the toilet) of the first-class coach. As the train rattled westwards that particular lamp either exploded or fell, starting a fierce fire in the tiny compartment.

Accounts of the fire's discovery vary. Conductor John Mitchell stated later that he saw a disturbance among some passengers which he took to be a fight; instead they were milling about the open door to the burning toilet. Attempts to stifle the blaze using cushions had no effect. Mitchell closed the door and shouted that everything was under control. That was not true. Nobody was quite sure about what to do, and panic was taking hold of everyone.

If two doors had been kept closed – the front door of the coach and the door to the toilet – the fire might have been confined to a small space. However, others opened the toilet door to attack the fire again, only to be driven back by flames. A strong draught whipped up the blaze, which spread rapidly down the coach. Few tried to break through to the smoker ahead of them; most crowded to the rear, jamming onto the platform and clinging to the railings until smoke, desperation or the crush of other passengers drove them to drop or jump off.

The problem, of course, was that without a bell cord there was no way to signal the engineer that he should halt the train. An attempt by a brakeman to uncouple the burning car failed. Conductor Mitchell was nearly frantic; among the passengers was one of his daughters. He ordered brakeman William Burke to climb over the other cars to reach the engine. Burke ventured out, then turned back, fearful of falling under the moving train.

Mitchell personally set out to alert the engineer. He climbed atop the second-class smoker, jumped onto the baggage car, leaped onto an oil tank car, and scrambled along it until he could jump to the next tanker. He repeated this dangerous performance until he could shout into the cab. Engineer George Williams promptly brought the train to a halt. It may have taken Mitchell two minutes to clamber from the burning coach to the head of the train, and Williams would have needed another minute to make a complete stop.

Once the train ground to a halt, brakeman Burke seized a lamp and started running back down the track, ready to flag down a following Windsor-bound train. Mitchell, unaware of Burke's action, also raced to halt the Windsor train. It was not far behind, but managed to stop some 40 car-lengths from the burning coach, which was now blazing furiously from end to end.

Komoka, 1874 – passengers leap from the burning train. Publications such as the *Canadian Illustrated News* relied on artists to reproduce events; their records are a rich source for modern historians. (National Archives of Canada C61133)

By all estimates the fire had begun when the train was about 4 miles (6 kilometres) from Komoka, and they had halted roughly 2.5 miles (4 kilometres) from that station. Dozens of people lay beside the tracks, some bruised, some battered from their escape.

Seven bodies, including those of a mother and her three-month-old infant, were taken from the death coach; London newspapers described the charred remains in lurid, sickening detail. Over the next two weeks three more passengers succumbed to their injuries.

An inquest opened in London on March 2. Considerable attention was paid to the lamp – the type of oil used, whether it had been securely clamped into place, whether or not it had been the object of tampering, perhaps by an inebriated passenger. There were many questions but no clear answers.

Less concern was given to the car coupling. Some witnesses said that it should have been easy to release the burning coach from the train. Obviously it had not been simple that night, and no probing ensued into the mechanics of couplings.

Understandably it was the matter of bell ropes that most occupied the inquest jury. The problem of ropes snagging on tanker cars was explained, but that was not allowed to stand as an excuse. Obviously the practice of disconnecting the only signalling device was widespread; the Windsor train immediately behind the Sarnia train had also been made up of tankers and coaches, and it too had been fitted with no bell rope that evening.

The jurors did not mince words in their findings. They urged that the government pass a law banning kerosene lamps on trains. They censured the Great Western Railway's management for not informing itself of the degree to which employees were following regulations. They recommended that Mitchell, Williams and Burke be charged with manslaughter for what was considered to be criminal negligence in not having the bell rope connected the whole length of the train. This last item stirred several newspaper editors; the *Sarnia Canadian* declared that the three men were being used as scapegoats; the *London Advertiser* agreed that the trio were fit subjects for a trial but suggested that the inquest jury had been unduly hard on the railway company.

The Middlesex Assizes met in London on May 5, 1874, with Mr. Justice Joseph C. Morrison presiding. His presence on the bench was interesting; until his appointment to the judiciary in 1862 Morrison had been a lawyer and politician with close links to railway companies, including the Great Western. The case list before him included several civil suits arising out of the Komoka tragedy as well as the manslaughter charges that had been laid against Mitchell, Williams and Burke.

In spite of his corporate railroad past, Morrison's address to the Grand Jury was a scrupulous description of the law. He cited the statutes that made it mandatory for passenger trains to carry devices for conductors to signal engineers; he quoted other laws that made clear the responsibilities of train crews. A close reading of his remarks suggest that he was leading the Grand Jury towards bringing in a "true bill" of indictment, which would have let the criminal cases go to trial. However, on May 8 the Grand Jury returned a conclusion of "no bill"; the manslaughter charges could go no further.

Modern readers, accustomed to litigation extending over years, may be interested to note the disposal of the various civil cases that had been brought against the company at this sitting. Most were handled in a single day, May 6. In Hooper vs. the Great Western Railway one Ebenezer Hooper was awarded $250 for minor injuries suffered in the February accident. The case of Munro vs. the Great Western Railway was more complex: Hugh Munro, a store clerk, had suffered severe, crippling injuries. He sought damages of $10,000; the company offered him $450; the civil jury awarded him $1,450 – a considerable sum (more than two years' wages) for those days.

Dunne vs. the Great Western Railway involved one W. Dunne whose 17-year-old daughter Harriet had been killed in the fire. The father sought $1,000 damages on the basis that he had lost the services that his daughter would have rendered him up to her 21st birthday. After considerable legal argument the jury concluded that the company owed not a penny to Mr. Dunne.

The last civil case related to the events of February 28 was that of Ryan vs. the Great Western Railway, heard on May 8. Mrs. T. Ryan had sustained injuries to her head and hip. These had healed, although she now endured headaches. The company offered $300 in damages; the jury increased the award to $600. Such were the scales of civil indemnity 127 years ago.

YAMASKA, Quebec

SEPTEMBER 28, 1875

The Richelieu, Drummond and Arthabaska Railroad, stretching from Sorel southeastwards into Quebec's Eastern Townships, was one of several small lines that were constructed in the 1860s and 1870s, surviving briefly before absorbtion by a larger company. This particular line was the creation of Louis Adélard Senécal, a prominent merchant, shipowner, entrepreneur and politician. In 1870-71 he had laid down 48 miles (77 kilometres) of track from Sorel to L'Avenir, using wooden rails with iron strapping on top. The first trains ran in 1872, but the rails immediately began breaking down. Senécal soon sold the firm for $100,000 to the South-Eastern Counties Junction Railroad Company. However, by 1875 he had renewed his association with the line by securing a contract to replace the wooden rails with iron ones and to extend the tracks to Acton, where they could tap the Grand Trunk's main line.

Each day one or two work trains would steam out from Sorel, carrying up to 100 men apiece on flatcars. The day would be spent in tearing out old rails and installing new ones. Then the trains would chug back to Sorel.

About 5:50 p.m. on the evening of June 28 just such a work train left the village of St. David and headed home. The engine with its tender was actually pushing the train – six flatcars on which some 75 workmen were riding. By 6:45 p.m. – in that distant age before daylight saving time – it was dark.

A brakeman, Edouard Lachapelle, was riding on the leading flatcar, peering ahead for any hazards. He had a lantern to signal the locomotive. Engineer Henri Gaudette was confident about the tracks and roadbed, and was running at between 8 and 12 miles per hour (13-19 km/hr). Riding on the tender were L.A. Senécal himself, Oscar C. Phelps (superintendent) and the conductor, Nathan P. Swan.

The workmen passed through Yamaska, a village 10 miles (16 kilometres) southeast of Sorel. A couple of miles further on the train crossed the Rivière David. Brakeman Lachapelle glimpsed something on the tracks some 60 feet (18 metres) ahead. He waved his lantern furiously, shouted a warning, then jumped. Almost everyone on the leading flatcar followed his lead. Engineer Gaudette saw the lantern signal, reduced steam and hit the brakes. He suspected that he was about to hit a cow.

His attempt to stop was too late. Two wooden timbers had been laid crossways on the track, and they derailed the first flatcar. This turned on its side and became a barrier; three following flatcars rammed into it and overturned; the fifth car derailed but remained upright; the sixth flatcar plus the locomotive and tender stayed on the tracks.

Ten workmen died in the crash and about 25 more sustained injuries that ranged from cuts and bruises to ghastly wounds. The Montreal *Daily Witness*, displaying typical contemporary journalistic taste, reported: "One poor fellow was rescued with his arm hanging to his body by a few shreds of flesh. Another man's feet were completely smashed out of shape."

Survivors tore up nearby fences to light bonfires, then pitched in to rescue their comrades, some of them trapped under capsized flatcars. Gaudette paused to assess the situation, then reversed his locomotive and steamed back to Yamaska. He returned quickly, bringing a doctor, a priest and salvage tools. In his absence, Louis Senécal rendered such aid and comfort as he could. The tracks were cleared, the injured loaded aboard a car, and the train sped to Sorel, arriving about 11:15 p.m.

The cause of the accident was obvious – the timbers laid across the rails. The *Daily Witness* expressed its horror: "The obstruction had been placed there by FIENDS IN HUMAN SHAPE whose hellish intention was but too surely accomplished." Suspicions turned towards some workmen who had been discharged a few days earlier; at least one had spoken bitterly of revenge.

A coroner's inquest was speedily convened under Ernest Turcotte and studied the incident in two days of sittings. Evidence was heard concerning the composition and speed of the train, as well as the condition of the roadbed and rails. An inspector testified that he had passed over the accident scene in a hand car at 5:30 p.m. and had found nothing out of order. However, the most significant evidence came from children.

An engraving of the nighttime Yamaska wreck of 1875. Another example of history portrayed in the *Canadian Illustrated News*. (National Archives of Canada C62930)

Denis Pepin, aged 12, and his brother Basil, 14, had previously placed coins, nails and wooden wedges on the rails to make passing cars bump as they passed. They had done so on the 27th and 28th. They did not admit to having placed any planks or timbers on the tracks. On September 30 the jurors reported their conclusions. The *Daily Witness* described them as follows:

> The jury after deliberation returned a verdict to the effect that the Railroad Company was in no way to blame, but that the accident had been caused by the action of some parties unknown. The Pepin boys, who had been arrested, were discharged, but strong suspicions are entertained that they caused the accident, not through malice but out of mischief.

Sabotage, vandalism and public mischief are closely related; the Yamaska crash may be regarded as the worst Canadian railway accident involving the element of deliberate, culpable action as opposed to human error.

* * *

Contemporary newspapers remind us of many disreputable aspects of the society they reported. The *Gazette de Sorel*, a small-town, thrice-weekly journal, resembled its big-city peers in many respects. It described in grim detail a September 30 rail excursion by reporters to the crash site; the area was still strewn with wreckage and blood stains were visible in spots. The paper expressed shock while doing nothing to shield readers from the horror of the place.

A short paragraph reported the rescheduling of a Sorel concert from October 1 to 5 as the community mourned its losses. Large newspaper advertisements in earlier issues of the *Gazette de Sorel* described who was involved in this event. The performers, then touring

Quebec to promote classical and operatic music, included pianist Calixa Lavallée, whose name figured prominently in publicity associated with the tour. Five years before composing "O Canada," Lavallée was famous – at least in his home province (he was a native of nearby Verchères) – as an itinerant musician.

TORONTO HIGH PARK, Ontario

JANUARY 2, 1884

The reader will have noticed that major train wrecks frequently were accompanied by earnest debates, assertions and denials about what had gone wrong and who was responsible. Such was not the case with the accident at Toronto High Park on the early morning of January 2, 1884. Blame was allocated quickly and admitted openly, though that did nothing to alleviate the catastrophe which wiped out 29 lives and left nine other men severely injured.

The chain of events began on the evening of January 1 when engineer Richard Jeffry* was called out to work on the Grand Trunk Railway (Great Western Division), the Grand Trunk having absorbed the Great Western in August 1882. Informed that he would ultimately be running a freight "light" (unloaded) into Toronto, Jeffry asked for a "pilot" (guide or experienced crewman) to take him over that route, with which he was unfamiliar.

He did not get one. Later the press latched onto this fact, suggesting that a pilot would have prevented disaster as surely as a pilot on a ship. Actually, in railway parlance of the day, a pilot had no authority to do anything aboard a train other than to advise the engineer about grades and roadbed conditions, the better to make appropriate steam pressure settings. Nevertheless, a railway pilot would have provided

* Contemporary newspapers also spelled his name as "Jeffrey."

another set of eyes and another brain which might have averted the tragedy – but it might have made no difference as well.

Instead of a pilot, Jeffry got an experienced conductor, George Barber. Throughout the night they operated in western Ontario with freight traffic, arriving in Hamilton in the early hours of January 2. There they received fresh orders – to take their light freight to the Queen's Wharf station in Toronto. The instructions looked simple enough, yet they were vague: "Run to Queen's Wharf, avoiding regulars." Later experts were to describe the situation thus: "The conductor went out taking his chances where and when he would meet trains."

"Avoiding regulars" was the chief concern. Tired though they were, Barber and Jeffry were accustomed to this sort of labour. It was not unusual for Grand Trunk crews to work 18-hour days. Studying the timetable, they noted that there was a mail and express train, Number 25, which they could expect to meet near Oakville. After that the way was clear. Another westbound train would not leave Toronto until 7:35 that morning.

It was there and then that the mistake was made. The timetable was not a simple document; it included a jumble of footnotes with various additional items – nature of certain stops, facilities at various stations – and in those footnotes was the information that several commuter or suburban trains running out of Toronto were also counted as "regulars." The first of these, from Queen's Wharf to Mimico, was due to leave at 6:40 a.m. Neither Barber nor Jeffry read the footnotes. Barber, the more experienced of the two, knew that commuter trains used the track they were taking, but on this occasion he simply forgot about them. Nothing in the next few minutes jogged his memory.

The light freight was scarcely a train at all, consisting only of the engine, tender, baggage car and caboose. It left Hamilton at 5:20 a.m., chugging through a howling blizzard. As it pulled out, a telegrapher passed a message to Toronto, advising of the freight's departure. The message was received but no action was taken. At 6:49 a.m. (nine minutes late) the commuter train chugged westward from Toronto, manned by John Kennedy (engineer), James Carter (conductor) and James Gasken (fireman).

It was a small train too – a small engine/tender combination (known as a "dummy") and two coaches carrying 43 workmen headed for the Toronto Bolt and Iron Works, a major foundry between High Park Station and Mimico. All but four or five of the passengers were in the forward coach. Once the commuter train pulled away no one seemed to think of the total picture – one which included two locomotives of vastly unequal weight steaming towards each other at a combined speed of roughly 50 miles per hour (80 km/hr), their crews mutually ignorant of one another, and vision obscured by the swirling snow,

There was one point where an accident might still have been prevented. That was at Mimico, the station where the commuter train was expected. It would have been possible for station personnel to halt any eastbound trains until the commuter arrived – possible except for the fact that the Mimico station was unmanned at that hour. No one was due to report there until about 7:30 a.m. The freight rattled through the station and started down a slope, speed building momentarily as it raced past the Toronto Bolt and Iron Works.

A few people, at the last moment, had premonitions. A watchman at the Bolt Works saw the freight passing and remarked to a friend, "The dummy will have a collision." John Donovan, a carpenter, was standing at the Bolt Works station, waiting for the commuter train to take him to Mimico. He too watched the freight pass. "Directly afterwards I heard the dummy whistle at the High Park crossing," he later declared. "As soon as I heard her whistle I knew there was going to be an accident, and I ran down the road."

In the cab of the dummy engine, John Kennedy saw the headlight of the approaching freight when it was barely 300 yards (280 metres) away; snow, curves and trees had all conspired to obscure his view. Kennedy whistled for brakes, shut off steam to prevent an explosion and made ready to jump. Gasken reached for the brakes, saw Kennedy leaping and the freight engine bearing down, and jumped to safety without delay. Aboard the freight locomotive the crew had not even enough warning to escape. The time was 6:57 a.m. – eight minutes out from the Queen's Wharf station.

The contest was utterly unequal and devastating to the commuter train. The Toronto *Mail* described what happened:

The heavy freight locomotive, backed by a tender fully laden with coal and water, together with the caboose and baggage car, dashed up against the comparatively light dummy. The boiler of the latter was carried completely off its wheels and, followed by the freight locomotive, smashed into the first passenger coach. So great was the velocity and consequent momentum of the ponderous freight engine that it mounted the trucks of the smaller engine, and running clean over them followed the boiler into the car. Strange to say the sides of the latter were almost intact. It was one of the most complete telescope accidents ever known. The wheels did not even leave the track and the rails were in no wise injured. As the boiler [of the dummy] dashed through the front of the car it carried its furnace with it, and in a few minutes the woodwork was in flames, and the poor unfortunates roasted alive. Bolts and rods, not of iron alone but wrought steel were bent and twisted like hair pins. The roof was splintered into kindling wood, and there was not a piece of it six inches square but was split or crushed. John Carrigan, who was sitting on [at?] the front of the car, was knocked through the roof, and although his body is full of splinters he is the only one not scalded or burnt, and will likely recover.

Within a few minutes men from the Bolt Works and nearby houses had converged on the scene to organize a bucket brigade. In the confusion no word of the accident was passed to the Toronto station and at 7:35 the No. 1 passenger train steamed out for Hamilton, its crew unaware of the carnage ahead. Approaching the wreck, it was met by several men waving and shouting wildly. The engineer halted his train. Once informed of the accident, he moved up slowly, loaded some casualties aboard, and backed up to the Queen's Wharf station. His return there was the first word of the collision to reach the main Toronto terminal.

At the wreck itself the first concern was to extinguish the flames. After that the work of rescue began, with axes, crowbars and jacks applied to the twisted, smoking debris. The grim work included sorting out the dead, dying and injured. "Tongue cannot tell the horrors of the three terrible hours that followed the collision," wrote the Toronto *Mail*, which then supplied nearly a third of a page in fine type describing the ghastly scenes at the collision site, in hospital and at the local morgue.

Fifteen men were killed outright or died shortly afterwards at the accident location. Ten more died that day in hospital, followed by two on the 3rd, one on the 7th, and one on the 10th. All but one of the victims were from the commuter train; Charles Thomas, fireman on

From the Toronto *Evening Telegram*, Wednesday January 2, 1884.

the freight, had been killed in the crash. The youngest casualties were three workers aged 13, 14 and 15. Most of the others left widows, children or various dependant relatives. James Kelly left a widow and nine children. Several families suffered multiple losses. William Turiff was killed on the spot; his brother Alexander died on the 7th. Three brothers named Macdonald were aboard the commuter train; two were killed and one was seriously injured. Two men named Aggett also died; the papers did not make clear whether or not they were related, although it is probable they were.

A coroner's inquest was opened immediately and continued with several adjournments until January 15, when the 15-man jury reported its findings in 12 paragraphs which covered every aspect of the accident. Not surprisingly they found that the direct cause of the accident had to be attributed to the engineer and conductor of the freight, Jeffry and Barber, for not having read their timetables more closely and hence failing to note that a commuter train was due, and a "regular" one at that. By way of mitigation the jury noted that both men had been working for 12 hours continuously, "too long a time considering the stormy character of the weather that night."

Having said that, the jury proceeded to spread as much responsibility around as possible. They noted Jeffry's previous request for a pilot and the ambiguous nature of his orders. They were critical of the Grand Trunk for having no staff at the Mimico station in the early morning, and for running the commuter train ten minutes late. The jury also noted that the large amount of traffic on the Toronto-Mimico run merited the introduction of double tracking.

Barber was committed for trial, charged with manslaughter, on January 15; Jeffry was similarly charged on the 16th. Justice moved swiftly. On the 22nd a Grand Jury returned a "true bill" against Barber. The trial itself began and ended on the 25th. Once again the events leading to the accident were reviewed, but this time the added element was legal discussion as to criminal intent. Since it was clear that Barber's mistake had put his own life in jeopardy there was obviously no malicious motive for him to misread the timetable. The jury returned a verdict of "not guilty."

One further detail is worth noting about this calamity – the public response. The Toronto High Park disaster had an element of tragic concentration; all but one of the dead came from a single factory, and most of the families involved knew one another. In an age when insurance was uncommon and government welfare unknown save on humiliating terms, private charity rushed to aid the families of those who had been killed or injured. John Holderness, proprietor of the Black Horse Hotel, donated 1,000 pounds (450 kilograms) of beef for relief, and a group of St. Lawrence Market butchers added 3,300 pounds (1,500 kilograms) from their stocks. Various organizations scheduled concerts and fund-raising drives. The Governor General sent $250; Colonel Casimir Gzowski put up $100; the Toronto Bolt and Iron Works raised $100. Donations large and small were listed in the newspapers. As of January 21 (the last day specific totals were published), $8,072.73 had been raised.

Yet even in charity, 19th-century society was semi-feudal in its outlook. Families entitled to benefits from the fund were required to have a representative at Toronto City Hall every Friday, *precisely* at 4:00 p.m. Another sign of this class-ridden age was a brief item in the Toronto *Mail* on January 5:

The Massey Manufacturing Co. will suspend work at their factory today, to enable the employees to attend in a body the funeral of the victims of the recent railroad disaster this afternoon. They will be accompanied by the Massey cornet band.

ST. THOMAS, Ontario

As of 1887 the oil capital of Canada was in London, Ontario, where Imperial Oil was but one of many new firms refining petroleum products from the Petrolia fields nearby. Thirty miles (50 kilometres) southward, Port Stanley on Lake Erie served as a harbour and resort centre for the metropolis. St. Thomas, nearer to Port Stanley than to London, was a city and rail centre through which lines passed on both the north-south and east-west axis. The Michigan Central Railway crossed the London and Port Stanley line virtually in the city centre.

About 6:40 p.m. on July 15, 1887, an excursion train pulled out of Port Stanley. It was composed of ten cars (nine coaches and a baggage car) and crowded with nearly 400 people, many of them children, who had attended church picnics that day. There was not enough seating; many were standing in the aisles and on the platforms between the coaches. Although it was running on London and Port Stanley tracks, this was actually a Grand Trunk train. At the controls was Henry Donnelly, aged 65, an experienced employee who had been working on British and Canadian railroads for 50 years as apprentice, fireman and engineer. His fireman was Harry Angles, while Richard Spettigue was conductor. Allan Davis was the front brakeman and John Mason was rear brakeman. Riding in the cab was George McMullen, a longtime friend of the engineer.

The trip to St. Thomas was accomplished rapidly; Donnelly was entering the town at roughly 40 miles per hour (60 km/hr). He passed a semaphore signal that hung limply down, indicating a clear track ahead. Actually it was a new signal, not yet in operation. Donnelly may or may not have known its true nature. Rules of the road stated that he should come to a full stop before crossing the Michigan Central's tracks; it was a regulation honoured more in the breach than in practice.

A Michigan Central freight with steam up began chugging westward, pulling a string of boxcars and 3,000-gallon tank cars, the latter filled with crudely refined petroleum. Two semaphore signals nearest the crossing advised northbound traffic to halt. The excursion train bore down, its speed slackening but still too fast. Donnelly applied air brakes. They did not respond.

Throughout the next few seconds the engineer spoke not a word, concentrating on the danger now posed by the freight before him. He whistled once, then blew a longer blast, calling for hand brakes. Angles (the fireman) and McMullen (the cab passenger) jumped from the engine. Donnelly reversed the wheels, but sheer momentum carried the train forward. Meanwhile, the brakemen, distracted by children on the platforms, were desperately applying hand brakes. It was all too late. At roughly 7:00 p.m., travelling at a rate estimated to be between 12 and 25 miles per hour (15-35 km/hr), the excursion train's locomotive blundered into a tank car. Within seconds, burning oil was pouring over the Grand Trunk locomotive, baggage car and forward coaches. Pandemonium took over from there. In the second coach was J.W. Westervelt with his family. Later he would describe the experience:

> We felt a sudden jar, but not sufficient to knock us out of our seats. The car swayed to one side, and seemed just about to turn over when it fell back on the rails all right again. I sprang to the window and looked out. The engine, baggage car and car next to

ours were already afire, although an instant had not passed since the crash. There was a stampede towards both ends of the car, and the doors became blocked. I clambered through the window and helped my family out.

Fearful as was the crash, the motion of the freight train dragged the forward part of the excursion train to the left, preventing a pile-up of coaches. Dazed passengers and scores of St. Thomas citizens braved the heat to extricate others from the wreck. The fire brigade rushed up and began playing water on the wreck, although hose pressure was very low.

Few people seemed to recognize the danger inherent in a second tank car, unruptured but adjacent to the one that had been struck and set alight. Confusion reigned as spectators milled around and various nearby buildings caught fire. Ten minutes after the crash the second tanker exploded with a roar. An oily fireball ballooned 100 feet (30 metres) into the sky, turning one fireman into a blazing statue. Windows were shattered four blocks away. Horses stampeded through the streets; a woman was run down and killed. Scores of people were scorched, and a few were badly burned. Onlookers fled in panic, tearing off burning coats or blouses as they ran. More than two hours passed before fire fighters had the flames under control.

When all the dead and injured had been tallied, 17 people were found to have died, 14 of them (including the engineer) from the Grand Trunk train. Four families bore the brunt of the catastrophe. John Baynes of London had not accompanied his family on the excursion that day; his wife Alice, aged 30, was killed, together with three daughters ranging in age from six years to 11 months; only a seven-year-old son, Wilber, escaped alive. S.G. Zealand of St. Thomas perished with his two-year-old daughter. Mrs. S. Fraine and her in-

(Facing page) Map of St. Thomas, showing where the tracks of the London and Port Stanley Railway crossed those of the Michigan Central (Canada Southern) in the centre of the town.

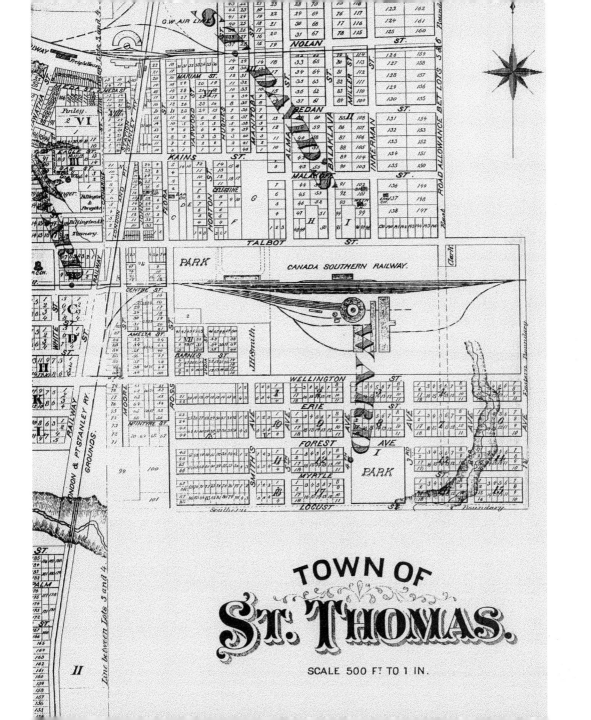

TOWN OF
ST. THOMAS.

SCALE 500 FT. TO 1 IN.

fant daughter, also of St. Thomas, were killed. So was Mrs. K. Smithers and her three-year-old son. Half-a-dozen firemen had been injured.

The immediate aftermath was as strange as the event had been terrifying. Souvenir hunters picked over the burned wreckage for two days. Among many observations, the London *Advertiser* included the following:

> Every other or third man met in St. Thomas seems to wear some mark of the explosion in the way of plasters, bandages, slings, etc. … Scores of hats were picked up near the scene of the wreck and explosion, where they had been lost by the owners in their mad flight to escape. The road bed for a block around is also littered with remnants of burned clothing torn from the backs of the injured spectators.

The mandatory coroner's inquest began on the 18th and sat until August 2. Conflicting evidence was to be expected; a particular bone of contention was whether engineer Henry Donnelly had been drunk. For every allegation that he had been under the influence, a witness could be found to deny it, and even to state that such would have been out of character for him. Indeed, much of the hostile testimony was vague and second-hand. Donnelly's own actions – whistling for brakes, reversing the engine, staying at the controls to the end – denoted a man taking all the right steps to avoid a collision.

Yet the collision had occurred. Why? Again, evidence was conflicting, including opinions as to how fast the excursion train had been moving. Overall, it did seem that Donnelly had been going too quickly for a built-up area and the approach to a familiar crossover; that much could be blamed on the dead engineer.

Many local citizens bristled at the actions of Robert Larmour, Assistant Superintendent of the Southern Division, Grand Trunk Railway. On the evening of the accident he had been summoned from London. Telephone and telegraph communications were broken between St. Thomas and Port Stanley. Larmour had given priority to on-the-spot relief, then to getting survivors to their destinations. He deliberately declined an offer from the Michigan Central Railway to send an engine to Port Stanley to bring other excursionists up to St. Thomas, choosing to delay their return until after midnight, although many had heard of the disaster and feared for relatives and friends who might have been involved. Inhabitants of St. Thomas regarded his decision as cruel and insensitive. The editor of the London *Advertiser* saw things in a different light:

The St. Thomas people seem unduly excited because the Assistant Superintendent of the Grand Trunk preferred to manage his own road instead of allowing them to do it for him. They say, imagine what the feelings of those left in Port Stanley must have been? Well, imagine what they would have been if they had been brought up as far as St. Thomas, into the smoke and fire, to see the charred and unrecognizable remains, which, for ought they might know, were those of friends or relatives, carried out of the burnt wreck. It would have had a very soothing effect on their feelings, indeed. Major Larmour should be commended for his actions on that terrible night. Immediately on receipt of the accident he hurried down himself on an engine to the scene, and as soon as a special could be made up it was sent for the people at St. Thomas. Those at Port Stanley were out of harm's way, and were left there until they could be brought home with safety.

The inquest did not seriously question the wisdom of having two lines intersect at a "diamond" junction, even though other juries had probed into the construction of lines and bridges. Nor did the St. Thomas jurors spend much time on the confusion that might have been caused by the semaphores; it will be recalled that two operable signals warned Donnelly that he should stop, but an inoperable semaphore was giving a clear-track signal.

Clearly the failure of the air brakes had been a major factor. They should have been examined by the fireman and conductor at Port Stanley; neither man had done so, although the latter had stopped and looked under the coaches. One man testified that the air brake on the leading coach differed markedly from that of the following coaches; it was suggested that the dissimilarity may have prevented the rest of the brakes from functioning. Theories were advanced that the brakes had become defective *after* leaving Port Stanley through the air lines developing kinks. There was no shortage of conjecture, yet nothing could be proven.

The verdict of the coroner's jury was a mixture of good sense and muddled thinking. It condemned the crowding of the train, but managed to link this to the drowning of a young woman at Port Stanley the same day! It declared that Donnelly had been unfit to serve as an engineer without stating why and in the face of evidence that he had been a sober, reliable employee. It referred to excessive train speeds in the city – and that was true enough. It concluded by declaring that Richard Spettigue's perfunctory look at the air brakes had been tantamount to criminal negligence. The unfortunate conductor was immediately arrested on a charge of manslaughter. On September 30, the Grand Jury of the Elgin County Assizes threw out the charge by finding "no bill" to the indictment. Thus concluded the story of the St. Thomas holocaust.

ST. GEORGE, Ontario

Parts breaking while the train was in motion – whether attributable to metal fatigue or inherent casting flaws – were mysteries that dogged early railroaders. Until the development of special equipment, such as the Sperry Rail Detector Car (1927) and heat-activated sensing devices, the only defence against such failures was rigorous and frequent inspections. Given the technology of the day, little was learned following the Desjardins Canal accident of 1857. The derailment at St. George, some 10 miles (16 kilometres) north of Brantford, Ontario, thus resembled the earlier tragedy not only in the cause but by involving a bridge.

By 1882 the Great Western Railway and the Grand Trunk Railway had merged, in spite of suspicions on the part of many that the result would represent monopoly at its worst. Some former terms and nomenclature survived the union. Such was the case of train No. 54, Grand Trunk Railway (Great Western Division), a regular passenger express running from Windsor to the Queenston Suspension Bridge. It was made up at Windsor; the train on February 27, 1889, consisted of the engine and tender, a baggage car, a Pullman sleeper, lounge car (or smoker), dining car and passenger coach. At London, according to practice, a new locomotive was placed on the train – No. 753 – and the engine crew was changed, with William Blackwell (engineer) and Henry Angles (fireman) coming on duty. It is not clear from contemporary accounts if Angles was the same "Harry Angles" who had been fireman aboard the Grand Trunk excursion train involved in the St. Thomas collision and fire.

This was not Blackwell's regular shift; the usual engineer had booked off sick and Blackwell had been called up at an hour's notice. He and Angles found No. 753 waiting for them with steam up. They set about their duties, Angles checking the coal feeders while Blackwell inspected his locomotive. He walked around it with oil cans and wrenches, topping off the oil cups and testing the crank pin keys. Everything was in order.

At 4:30 p.m. the train pulled out of London on time. The trip continued smoothly, with scheduled stops at Ingersoll, Woodstock, Princeton and Paris. Water was taken on at Woodstock and more oil applied. Still nothing seemed out of the ordinary. They left Paris at 5:49 p.m., steaming eastward. No stop was scheduled at St. George itself, a village beside a deep, wide creek which was spanned by a wooden trestle bridge some 60 to 80 feet (18.2 to 24.4 metres) high at the centre.

St. George had a siding located slightly to the east of the station and west of the bridge; the western switch was some 1,223 feet (373 metres) west of the bridge and the eastern switch was 353 feet (107 metres) from the bridge. All subsequent witnesses testified that the roadbed, switches, tracks and bridge were in good repair. Nevertheless, minutes after the train left Paris, and was travelling at some 45 miles per hour (72 km/hr), a main right driving wheel on the locomotive lost its steel tire; the driving rods broke and the engine blundered onto and over the bridge, spreading the rails as it went. Cars ran off the track, tore through the bridge beams, then uncoupled and toppled through to the creek bed below.

The dining car and passenger coach both took the fatal plunge. The latter turned a complete somersault and landed flat on its carriage with a resounding crash. The dining car fell end-first and finished up almost vertically, the top part leaning against the bridge pier. The parlour car hung out over the bridge but remained on the span.

G.C. Eden, Woodstock's town clerk, had left the passenger coach for the smoker, accompanied by three friends. One of the latter, A.M. Frances (also of Woodstock), had returned to his regular car. Eden subsequently recounted the accident to a reporter for the Toronto *Mail:*

I was in the smoking car, and feeling an unusual jolting in the car I turned to the window and saw we were just passing over a high bridge, when I immediately became aware that the hind carriage had left the track. I rushed out of the car and down the embankment, and there stood the car which had run immediately behind the smoker, standing squarely on its bottom, the inside presenting a terrible scene. Stoves, seats and people were all huddled together, and but two escaped uninjured – one a woman of about twenty, the other a man of about the same age.

C.A. Deslisle of Toronto had also been in the smoker when the car began shaking violently, derailed, but continued moving forward. He was ready to leap from the door when he found himself looking down into the deep ravine. "Shall we jump?" he shouted to a brakeman. "Not much!" was the reply, "as long as the old thing hangs to the rails."

A common feature of major disasters was a supply of stories relating to uncommon escapes and factors that markedly affected the casualty toll. In this accident the dining car had held only seven passengers and a waiter at the moment of derailment. Supper had been called barely minutes before. Had the train come to grief on the bridge even five minutes later the diner would have had many more people in it.

The newspapers reported the good fortune of a Brantford man named Yates. He was thrown from the coach, landed unhurt and

ST LOUIS EXPRESS - SMASH-UP

FEBRUARY 27 · 1889.

W.H. Margetts

ST GEORGE'S · ONT

walked to nearby Harrisburg. From there he caught another train to his home town where he telephoned friends that he was all right.

Engineer Blackwell described the wreck as seen from the front of the train. Even at the inquest, his account was not altogether coherent; he may have "frozen" at the controls. As he passed the St. George

A contemporary lithograph of the St. George wreck. (National Archives of Canada C47921)

siding, half-way between the two switches, he suddenly realized that things were amiss:

> I noticed something give way under where I was standing. I was in the cab. I do not know what it was. I noticed splinters thrown up, and the tire was thrown off, I think, between the two sidings [he meant switches]. I did not do anything. I did not reverse the engine. I did not put on the air brakes. I did not blow the whistle; it was impossible to stay in the cab. I ran to the rear of the engine, and the fireman jumped off. I could not stop the train if I did reverse; in that distance it would have no power to stop the train. The trailing wheel, the tire, and the left driving wheel were off on the other side of the bridge. I could apply the air brakes, reverse the engine, and give all the power I could to stop a train if necessary but could not in this case do anything. I could stop the train in about four or five hundred yards.

Charles Stiff, superintendent of the line, subsequently went over the scene of the accident. He picked up the broken tire in a field, and estimated that it had come off the locomotive some 50 yards (46 metres) short of the bridge. From marks on the rails he concluded that the fracture itself had occurred about 150 yards (137 metres) west of the bridge. He agreed that the train would have needed 500 yards (457 metres) to come to a full stop, so there would have been nothing that Blackwell could have done once the tire broke.

Arthur Smith, assistant mechanical superintendent for the company, examined the broken tire and was hard put to distinguish any faults or cracks from marks inflicted during the accident itself. The fractures were not rusty, suggesting that they had appeared only recently or had resulted from the crash. The cracks, in any case, were on the inside of the tire and would have been undetectable so long as the tire remained on the wheel.

On March 1 the coroner's jury returned its verdict. It could find no fault with the railway's personnel and made only one recommendation – that trains should slow to about 12 miles per hour (18 km/hr) when approaching the bridge. One wonders at this suggestion, for the speed near or on the bridge seems to have been unrelated to the cause of the accident itself. Ten people had died and 32 had been injured in a tragedy which, given the technology of the age, was well-nigh unavoidable.

HAMILTON, Ontario

APRIL 28, 1889

The St. George wreck was soon followed by another. This one occurred close to the location of the Desjardins Canal disaster 32 years earlier. It involved an eastbound Grand Trunk express travelling from Windsor to Hamilton and thence to the Niagara bridges. The train was carrying between 105 and 120 passengers, most of them Americans headed for New York to celebrate the centennial of George Washington's presidential inauguration. Strung out behind the locomotive and tender were two baggage cars, a lounge car, two day coaches, a sleeping car, another day coach and three further sleeping cars.

The layout of tracks at the western end of Burlington Bay was fairly complex, for the line had to follow trench cuttings through limestone as it descended the Niagara escarpment. At a point between Dundas and Hamilton a switch divided the tracks, one set of rails going to Toronto while the other made for Hamilton. An eastbound train would complete a sharp right-hand turn, cross the switch and then make another sharp turn – left if heading to Toronto, right if bound for Hamilton – before entering another rock cutting. A high embankment carried the line across a small swamp; the switch and the beginnings of the diverging rail lines were on this elevated portion of track.

It was 7:15 a.m. on April 28, 1889, as the train approached the area, 6 miles (10 kilometres) from Hamilton. Although he was running 15 minutes late, engineer Joseph Watson may not have been exceeding the normal speed; a company rule of two months standing forbade crews from making up lost time by speeding. This day, however, the tracks were slick with rain. Given the situation – a heavy load, greasy rails, a downhill grade – it seems probable that he was going too fast on this particular day, whether on schedule or not. His train negotiated the first curve, crossed the switch at high speed and entered the second curve. At this point the locomotive jumped the tracks.

Driven by its own momentum, the engine crossed 195 feet (60 metres) of open ground before hitting a wooden water tank that disintegrated in a flash. The locomotive slewed over on its back. The tender was catapulted over the engine, spilling its coal as it flew. The baggage cars derailed and hurtled past the locomotive. The smoking car crashed into the engine and in turn telescoped the car behind it. Succeeding cars derailed; only the last two remained on the tracks. The Hamilton *Daily Spectator* took up the story:

Of the scene that followed no coherent account can be obtained from the survivors. Amid the escaping steam and the blinding rain, the screams of the injured arose from the awful mound of debris. The survivors at once became a band of rescuers, and the men worked like tigers to get at the victims in the wreck. Those scattered about were first secured and carried out of harm's way, but wails and screams and the groans of the dying came from the inner part of the wreck.

Watson and his fireman, Edward Chapman, had been thrown clear as the engine capsized; their escape was described as "miraculous." The worst carnage would be in the forward smoker and day coach; a dozen injured passengers were hauled from the splintered cars. A woman who refused to be identified performed heroically, tugging at timbers and dragging out a passenger even as flames threatened to set her clothes on fire. Baggageman James Welch, although injured, attacked the wreckage with such gusto that several passengers subsequently wrote letters commending his courage and leadership.

The rescue efforts ended abruptly when the wreckage caught fire. Coal oil from a dozen broken lamps, possibly ignited by spilled embers from the locomotive's firebox, provided the first fuel. The coaches, reduced to kindling in the crash, burned easily. Rescuers in the act of pulling out victims drew back as flames shot up in their faces. In spite of the rain and the water fetched by bucket brigade up the embankment from the swamp, the fire spread quickly from car to car. Only the last two sleepers, uncoupled and still on the tracks, could be pushed clear of the conflagration.

Word of the accident spread through Hamilton and nearby villages. Hundreds of spectators appeared, stand-

ANOTHER HORROR

Terrible Railway Accident at the Fatal Junction Cut.

A Catastrophe Eclipsing All Recent Disasters in the Province.

Twenty People Killed and Over a Dozen Injured, Some Badly.

Eighteen Unfortunates Imprisoned in the Wreck and Burned to Death.

Most of the Victims Americans Going to the Washington Centennial.

The Train Takes Fire and is Destroyed, xcept Two Sleepers.

The Accident Caused by the Train Jumping the Track at the Curve.

Interviews With the Survivors and Description of the Wreck.

No Canadians Among the Dead or Injured Passengers.

The Killed.

RUDOLPH J. EDERER, of Chicago.
L. S. GURNEY, of New York.
EIGHTEEN PERSONS, whose remains have not yet been identified.

The Injured.

HAMILTON CLARK, 147 West Ohio street, Chicago, Ill.—double fracture of the right leg; head cut; bruised on the arms. Serious

ANTONIO MARTZ (Italian)—cut in the back of the head. From Wisconsin, on his

ing on rocky ledges that offered an excellent view. "The plateau above was black with buggy tops," wrote a reporter, who estimated that more than a thousand onlookers were present at any one time.

It was 2:00 p.m. before officials began poking into the smoking ruins, and then the true horror began to dawn. Charred bodies were discovered, one after another, until 18 had been retrieved. Some, burned beyond recognition, would never be identified; the names of others would be determined through items such as engraved watches found on their persons.

A coroner's inquest was convened that day and continued, with several lengthy adjournments, until June 10. Gathering evidence was complex and not fully satisfactory. The most knowledgeable witnesses were also the people with the greatest at stake – employees of the Grand Trunk itself, ranging from track-walkers and switchers to section supervisors and the company's general manager, the ubiquitous Charles Brydges. There was little opportunity to call independent witnesses.

An example of the difficulties encountered was the determination of the train's speed. Although one passenger signed a deposition claiming that they had been going 50 miles per hour (80 km/hr), the opinion of most witnesses was that the express had been moving at closer to 25 miles per hour (40 km/hr). Was this rate excessive for the circumstances? Grand Trunk employees were almost unanimous in their opinion that the curve and switch could be negotiated easily at that pace. The inquest jurors did not agree; in their report they said that 20 miles per hour (30 km/hr) was too great for a curving, downhill track with a switch, suggesting that 15 miles per hour (25 km/hr) would be a more prudent speed. Their opinion may have represented excessive caution on the part of laymen; company personnel, having nothing to gain from derailments brought on by unsafe speeds, prob-

(Facing page) Headlines from the *Hamilton Spectator*, April 29, 1889. Multiple layers of headlines were a feature of 19th-century newspapers.

ably knew best about the capacities and limitations of the tracks. All the same, the presence of wet rails may have meant that 25 miles per hour was too fast on that particular morning.

The rail line and switch appeared not to have been faulty. Questions were raised about the possibility of a rail having been broken or twisted. However, the line had seen the passage of a dozen trains a day for years; a freight had been over the spot only 30 minutes before the express arrived. All this indicated a serviceable track.

As the inquest progressed, the locomotive gradually emerged as the principal suspect. Evidence was hard to find. Hundreds of spectators and souvenir hunters had descended on the site; it was feared that relevant items might have been picked up or trampled into the mud. The company's own efforts to repair the line within a day might also have obliterated material evidence. A broken bolt discovered on the tracks suggested mechanical failure; a broken axle and wheel flange on the engine hinted that the cause lay there – but had these cracked *before* the derailment or *after*? The jurors accepted the former as being the most probable, blaming the accident on "the breaking of the flange of the left leading wheel of the engine truck, which break allowed the wheels to leave the track at the switch." Nevertheless, they expressed their frustration in the investigation when they put forth the following recommendation:

that the government take such action as may be necessary to ensure a full and complete inspection by a competent person in all cases where there has been loss of life through accident before anything whatsoever had been removed or touched than what may be necessary to rescue bodies from the wreck. Had this been followed the jury would have come to a verdict with much more ease and certainty.

If the inquest jury was correct, the Hamilton wreck was precipitated by the same culprit – metal fatigue – that had wrought havoc at Desjardins Canal, Shannonville and St. George, and would be related in kind to the root cause of the Spanish River wreck of 1910. The jury did not comment on the causes of the fire, but the Hamilton *Daily Spectator* did. An editorial pointed to the dangers posed in an accident by oil lamps and coal-fired stoves, urging that means be adopted "to heat the cars with steam and light them with electricity." Similar views had been expressed following the Komoka railway fire of 1874; 15 years later, little had changed. Indeed, new technology would be no absolute guard against fire, as subsequent wrecks – notably the 1947 disaster at Dugald, Manitoba – would demonstrate.

CRAIG'S ROAD, Quebec

JULY 9, 1895

The shrine at Ste. Anne de Beaupré, east of Quebec City, had become a well known site of pilgrimage by the late 19th century. Visitors coming by train normally went to Lévis, crossed the St. Lawrence by boat (there would be no bridge until 1917) and were then transported by carriage or boat to the village with its sanctuary.

Late on July 8, 1895, two special Grand Trunk Railway trains were assembled at Sherbrooke with Lévis as their destination. They were filled with pilgrims headed for Ste. Anne de Beaupré. The leading train carried 314 passengers. Its crew included engineer Alexander Ferguson, conductor Abraham Dionne, sleeping car conductor J.P. Morewood and three brakemen. It had a strong white headlight and two (some said three) red lights at the rear.

The second train, carrying about 300 further pilgrims, had as its engineer 50-year-old Hector McLeod. He had spent half his life in the service of the Grand Trunk. Everyone considered him to be a sober, reliable man, although he was troubled by asthma. McLeod and his crew were running under general orders which stated, among other things, that trains would slow down, sounding bells and whistles, when passing through stations, even if no stop was intended. Apart from that, McLeod was advised to try to maintain a healthy spacing – roughly the distance from one station to another – from the lead train, to watch for track signals and to keep a special lookout for the red lamps at the rear of the first special. It was assumed that McLeod's train would be some 30-40 minutes behind Ferguson's. Subsequent evidence indicated that, although the spacing varied, the two trains generally had some 20-35 minutes running time separating them.

The weather was important in what followed. Visibility was good, but it was a very warm night. Crews sweated in the locomotive cabs, where it was fiercely hot. The men resorted to water and jars of tea to slake their thirst.

About 2:28 a.m. on July 9, the leading train pulled into St. Agapit station. The crew received an order to advance to Craig's Road station, some 18 miles (29 kilometres) short of Lévis, where they would halt on the main line. A westbound freight train would meet them there and take to the siding, thus permitting the excursion train to carry on. It was a routine "pass" order. At 2:32 a.m. engineer Ferguson opened the throttle and chugged out. McLeod's train went through about 2:50 a.m. At that point the trains had a relatively narrow 18-minute spacing.

The leading train reached Craig's Road at about 2:55 a.m. There were no station hands about at this hour, so the train crews set the signals, showing red in both directions. Ten minutes later the freight arrived, halted, then began moving onto the siding. It was discovered

(Facing page) Headlines from the *Globe*, Toronto, July 10, 1895.

that some rolling stock blocked the siding, and the freight halted with four of its boxcars still on the main line. The pilgrim train, standing about 300 feet (90 metres) from the eastern switch, could not advance until this minor muddle was sorted out.

It was about 3:06 a.m. Dawn was just beginning to tint the eastern horizon. Conductor Dionne looked back. About 1.5 miles (2 kilometres) off he could see the second excursion train bearing down on his own. It did not appear to be slowing; no bells or whistles were sounding. Dionne was alarmed. He sent a brakeman with a lantern to run down the road and try to flag the train. Then he signalled to his own engineer to move forward. Up in the cab, Ferguson could not see what was happening, but he obeyed. His train began to inch ahead, although the freight cars still blocked his way.

The brakeman sent to warn the second train, identified later only as "Wheeler," was standing beside the track, close to the western switch, shouting and swinging his lantern as the second excursion train rumbled by him. It had not slowed a bit since Dionne had first spotted it; its whistle and bells were still silent. Running at some 35 miles per hour (53 km/hr) the second excursion locomotive ploughed into the heavy sleeping car in the rear of the leading train.

The carnage was terrible; 13 people were killed on the spot, and another died within hours. The injured totalled 38. The Pullman sleeper rammed and was wedged inside the coach ahead, which in turn telescoped the rear of the next coach up. The force of the crash threw the speeding locomotive on its side. Station windows were broken by flying debris.

Death struck brutally yet randomly. Charles Bédard, a Richmond businessman, was killed instantly in the Pullman; his two children emerged with minor scratches; his seven-year-old daughter fell through the floor of the sleeper and crawled out between its wheels.

DISREGARDED THE SIGNALS

Terrible Accident on the Grand Trunk Near Levis.

THIRTEEN PERSONS KILLED.

Rear-End Collision of Excursion Trains.

The Engineer of the Second Section Ran Past the Signals — Suffering and Heroism.

Levis, July 9.—(Special.)—Of the pilgrims from points in the eastern townships bound for the shrine of Ste. Anne de Beaupre to be cured of various ailments thirteen met a horrible death this morning early in a railway smash-up at Craig's Road, on the G.T.R., fourteen miles out of Levis, and 30 or more were badly injured. The Grand Trunk in the summer-time is in the habit of running special excursion trains to Point Levis on the route to Ste. Anne de Beaupre, and large numbers of people living along the route, as, for example, in Sherbrooke, Danville and Arthabaska, take advantage of them, and organise themselves into excursion parties, under the direction of their priests, for the purpose of paying their devotions at the shrine. On this particular excursion the number of pilgrims amounted to 550, and they were being carried by two trains. One of these, consisting of nine coaches, left Sherbrooke at 9.30 o'clock, and another of six left Norton Mills at 8.30 o'clock. They reached Craig's Road, fourteen miles west of Point Levis, at about a quarter past 3 this morning. At that time the nine coaches were ahead, and there was an interval of 20 minutes between the two trains. The first train stopped, and the semaphore was set up at "danger." The last car was the Pullman "Balmoral," in which were the priests, etc., in charge of the party, and it was in

Morewood, the Pullman conductor, had seen the second train coming for at least a minute before the crash; he came out with cuts and bruises.

The toll could have been worse. Dionne's quick thinking had set his train in motion; that lessened the force of the impact. Engineer Ferguson applied his brakes only when it was necessary to avoid ramming the freight cars ahead of him.

Word of the wreck flashed down the telegraph wires. Officials from Lévis reacted swiftly. A relief train with six doctors arrived about 90 minutes after the crash, and a wrecking train followed. By 10:00 a.m. the survivors – injured and unhurt – had been evacuated to Lévis and Quebec. By 3:00 p.m. the line was clear for traffic, although wreckage still littered the area.

A searching inquest followed. Two important witnesses were missing, McLeod and his fireman. Both had been killed in the wreck. It appeared that the engineer had set his brakes just before the impact and had been preparing to jump when the crash occurred.

Certain facts were established. All parties, including crewmen aboard the second excursion train, stated that the following train had sounded no bells or whistles. The train had not slowed appreciably. The Craig's Road station signals facing west had shown red. That crucial point was confirmed by crewmen aboard both passenger trains. The freight crew reported that they had encountered a red signal when arriving at Craig's Road; it was likely that if the eastern signal had been properly set, the western one had also been turned correctly. The stricken train had clearly displayed red lanterns from its rear. There was simply no good reason why Hector McLeod should have driven his locomotive into the lead train.

Lawyers questioning witnesses turned up some odd facts. Railway policy did not require eye examinations of employees. Conductor

Dionne was colour blind. Engineer Ferguson had had his eyes checked only once in 23 years with the company.

It was Ludger Perrault who gave the only testimony that suggested a reason for the crash. Perrault ran a hotel only a hundred yards from the station at Arthabaska. He stated that on the evening of July 8, Hector McLeod had entered the hotel, purchased a quart of beer and poured it into his tea jar. McLeod had been on duty – he was wearing his engineer's overalls – and thus his buying the beer was a violation of company rules.

Hector McLeod may not have been drunk that night – one witness had smelled the body and thought it had an odour of tea – but he may have been asleep. The combined factors of alcohol and a hot cab would have combined to lull him into drowsiness. His fireman, who should have been keeping a lookout, obviously had provided no assistance.

The coroner's jury made several recommendations. It suggested incorporation of an improved block signal system into the line. It advocated yearly eye examinations for trainmen. As to blame, it fixed this firmly on the running crew of the second train; the accident had been caused by "negligence and carelessness on the part of employees of the said company."

VICTORIA, British Columbia

MAY 26, 1896

Strictly speaking, an account of the Point Ellice bridge disaster does not belong in a book devoted to railroad accidents. It involved only one item of rolling stock, an electric tramcar. Nevertheless, the tragedy, which ranks as North America's worst street railway disaster, has been described in only one previous book.* By stretching the rules

* Derick Pethwick, *British Columbia Disasters*, Stagecoach Press, Langley, British Columbia, 1978.

set down in the Introduction, we may include the tale for those who have missed its telling elsewhere.

The harbour of Victoria, British Columbia, narrows into the Inner Harbour and then Portage Inlet. Three bridges connect Victoria itself with Esquimalt to the west. Of these, the Point Ellice bridge dates from 1861; the original structure was followed by another in 1872. This was succeeded in turn by a third bridge, constructed in 1885. The new link was 645 feet (196 metres) long, divided into four spans resting on concrete piers. The bridge itself was made largely of wood (timbered frame, planked deck) with iron braces. When assembled it carried pedestrians and horse-drawn carriages. A new element was introduced in 1890 – steel rails and heavy electric streetcars operated by the Consolidated Electric Railway Company.

On May 24, 1893, the bridge roadway suddenly sagged about 3 feet while Tramcar No. 16 was crossing. Motorman Harry Talbot brought the car safely across, but the structure was suspect. Victoria City Council budgeted $1,000 for work aimed at repairing and strengthening the bridge; this included removal of several rotting flooring planks.

Once the work was done, officials declared the Point Ellice bridge safe. All the same, tramcar operators were ordered to maintain a minimum 100-foot (30-metre) spacing between cars when on the bridge. Drivers of horse-drawn vehicles were advised to cross at a walk so as not to set up damaging vibrations. Not all did so. One eminent citizen complained that fast-driven carriages set the bridge shaking so violently that pedestrians had to grasp handrails and bridge struts to retain their footing. The city responded by despatching police to catch and fine reckless drivers. Sometimes an inspector checked the bridge, watching from a boat as vehicular traffic passed over, or boring 1.5-inch (37-mm) holes in the timbers to test their soundness. Once drilled, the holes were left uncapped, collecting water and encouraging rot.

In 1896, Queen Victoria's birthday, May 24, fell on a Sunday, which had to be observed with all the sobriety and piety reserved for the Sabbath. Instead, Monday and Tuesday were dedicated to picnics, excursions and fireworks. Celebrants in Victoria and Esquimalt jammed streetcars to their limits and beyond.

There was to be a military parade and sham battle at Esquimalt at 2:00 p.m. on the 26th, so hundreds of people headed there. At 1:50 p.m. two tramcars were running from Victoria towards the Point Ellice bridge. Car No. 6, a relatively light vehicle, was in the lead, followed by car No. 16, a much heavier machine weighing about 11 tons empty. On this day it was crowded to capacity, with every seat taken, the aisle full and several people standing on the front and rear platforms, thus violating posted safety regulations. There were an estimated 142 passengers aboard.

Car No. 16 was the same vehicle that had triggered the bridge scare of May 1893. Its crew consisted of George Farr (motorman) and Harry Talbot (conductor); the latter had also been present at the incident three years before. This accident would have more than its share of ironies.

As car No. 6 rattled over the second span, its conductor felt an unusual bumping; he believed that the vehicle's suspension system was faulty. Back in car No. 16, motorman Farr slowed to maintain the regulation spacing between tramcars. Subsequent evidence was conflicting. Some said that car No. 6 had left the span before No. 16 started upon it, while others declared that the two vehicles were at opposite ends of the span. There was no question that car No. 16 shared the span with several pedestrians, a cyclist, a two-horse carriage and two one-horse carriages.

One horse, sensing danger, bolted, wheeled about and galloped back towards the city. The tramcar had now advanced some 40 feet (12 metres) onto the second span. Suddenly there was a loud crack. Car No. 16 sagged on the tracks, dropping a foot and a half, but it kept moving forward. There followed a second, louder crack. Abruptly, the bridge collapsed into a harbour that was flooded by high tide.

Here was no Desjardins Canal, where a locomotive went through a bridge. In this case, the whole span went down, carrying car No. 16 with it. The bridge section apparently parted from its Esquimalt-end pier first, then ripped away from its pier on the Victoria side. The mass sank quickly, but car No. 16 did not go to the bottom. It settled on a jumble of bridge wreckage, 10 feet (3 metres) from the harbour floor and tilted towards its right side.

The Point Ellice bridge in happier days, before tracks were installed for tramcars. (BC Archives C-00463)

Survivors remembered the crash, the sudden drop, darkness and the water rising about them. Many could not recall how they escaped; their next conscious experience was rescue on the surface. Some had glass fragments in their clothes, evidence of their having slipped through broken windows. John Armstrong remembered struggling with three others to get out by a single window. It is entirely possible that underwater panic resulted in some passengers kicking others senseless in the battle for the exits.

Among those aboard were three sisters, Sophie, Alice and Inez Smith. The first two had found places aboard the car. Inez, unable to find a seat, was standing on the rear platform when the bridge collapsed. She fought clear of the car and swam to shore; Sophie and Alice were trapped inside and drowned.

Mr. and Mrs. E.H. Carmichael, together with their daughter and her escort, had intended to board No. 16 together. When it was evident that the car was packed, the group split up. The younger couple took car No. 6 and escaped the disaster; the elder Carmichael couple perished.

James Wilson had been driving his horse and carriage across the bridge, with his four children. The elder Wilson and three youngsters survived, but his five-year-old son died, apparently of fractures when a beam fell on him. The horses, their harness tangled in the wreckage, drowned. By a further irony, James Wilson was a street and bridge inspector for the city of Victoria.

Sailors working at a nearby wharf were the first rescuers on hand. Two genteel ladies took a rowboat to the scene and saved seven people, some of whom were clinging to wooden bridge wreckage. Two of the people they retrieved were probably Lula and Stella Wall. The Victoria *Colonist* reported: "Miss Stella was insensible when she rose to the surface and for some time was buoyed up by her younger sister,

until rescued. It was not until late on Tuesday night that she regained consciousness."

The papers were filled with stories of escape and heroism. Another tale concerned Eliza Woodhull, who "broke through the window nearest to her while the car was under water and, keeping hold of the two children who were with her, kept them and herself afloat until all three were picked up by one of the fleet of rescue boats."

The death toll was quickly established – 55 fatalities, including the Wilson child who had been riding in a carriage plus Frank James, the cyclist who had been on the bridge. Victoria mourned on a grand scale. Newspapers sported black borders, theatres closed, a dance was

The scene at the Point Ellice bridge following its collapse. (BC Archives A-02737)

postponed five days and a choir put off weekly practice. Meetings were cancelled, including political rallies and a WCTU conference.

Investigation of the Point Ellice bridge disaster involved two coroner's juries and a provincial inquiry. The poor state of the structure came out quickly – the rotting timbers were mute but powerful witnesses. One juror tested a timber by inserting his knife and watched it sink effortlessly to the hilt. Experts testified that bolt holes in the timbers as well as test holes bored to check their strength had been points of rapid decay. One man reported that the bridge had been warped by 7 inches (17 centimetres) – the south side was higher than the north side by that much – but that may or may not have been important in the matter of induced vibration.

Throughout these investigations there was considerable shuffling to avoid blame. Officials of the provincial government, which had built the bridge, said it was the responsibility of the city, which had maintained it since 1892. City bureaucrats argued that in law it was still a provincial structure. They also stated that, by the standards of the day, the bridge had been thoroughly checked, and that there had been no reports made to suggest that it was anything but safe. It had, after all, been carrying loads, some heavier than car No. 16, for many years. Should the city be blamed if a bridge that had stood for 4,000 days collapsed on the 4,001st?

The coroner's jury that reported on June 12, 1896, was surprisingly harsh with the Consolidated Electric Railway Company, to which it assigned primary blame for having allowed a tramcar loaded beyond regulation limits to pass upon the bridge. The city of Victoria was described as having shown contributory negligence in that it had poorly inspected and maintained the structure.

The disaster resulted in no fewer than 72 civil actions being brought against the city of Victoria. The corporation put up a stiff

The tramcar hauled up on shore after the Point Ellice bridge collapse.
(BC Archives C-06135)

legal battle. Two cases were deemed to be especially important. Marion R. Patterson and Martha Long, both widowed by the tragedy, won in British Columbia courts, the former being awarded $15,000 and the latter $20,000. The city appealed these decisions to the Judicial Committee of the Privy Council. That august body, sitting in London, England, was to remain the final court of appeal for Canadian civil law cases until 1949. In the Patterson and Long cases, the Privy Council heard arguments in early June 1899 and handed down its rulings on the 9th of that month.

The city had continued its attempt to evade liability by two legal devices. The first was its continued claim that the province, not the municipality, was responsible for the bridge. A British Columbia statute declared that roads and bridges were provincial property until such time as a municipality took control, and that such control was indicated by the passing of an appropriate by-law. The city argued that it had never enacted such a by-law prior to the accident and hence liability lay elsewhere.

Law Lords of the Privy Council did not accept this line of defence. They pointed out that the city had effectively been cleaning, maintaining and inspecting the bridge with municipal employees and funds for four years before its fall. After the accident, without passing any other by-law, the city had enacted regulations for tramcars and other traffic on all city bridges, apparently assuming that the corporation had control and responsibility.

The other defence argument, based upon legal precedent, was that even if the bridge had been the responsibility of the city, a municipality was not liable for damages arising out of misfeasance (that is, incorrect performance of its duties). The English judges, however, took a harsh view of this defence. They implicitly adopted the plaintiffs' views that the boring of holes and leaving them to collect water was calculated to rot this beam; that for a period of four years this beam was left in that condition, collecting water and … diffusing a state of rottenness all through the beam. That action was done by an officer of the corporation, upon its direction, and paid for by them. That would, under ordinary circumstances, be ample evidence to justify the verdict which was ultimately found against the corporation.

The judges suggested (though they did not explicitly state) that the city had been guilty of malfeasance (not mere incorrect performance of duties, but conducting an operation in an entirely unsuitable and dangerous manner – a civil equivalent of criminal negligence). Victoria's civic politicians were stunned by the decision. Including court costs, lawyers' fees and damages, the corporation had paid out $50,000 in the Patterson and Long cases. At the time it appeared that damages from all litigants might total one million dollars. Fortunately for the city not all plaintiffs were in the same category as Mrs. Long and Mrs. Patterson – widows bereft of breadwinners and responsible for young children. Litigants who had merely lost a spouse, child or distant relative, or had sustained only personal injuries, could be paid off more cheaply. In the end, the municipal corporation settled claims that totalled $150,000.

A temporary bridge was thrown across the harbour at Point Ellice. This served until 1904 when a new four-span bridge was built. This was replaced in 1957 by the structure that stands today. No monument, plaque or cairn commemorates the 1896 tragedy.

MURRAY HILL, Ontario

The Grand Trunk Railway figured in yet another major crash in mid-November 1898. The tragedy arose from two human errors – one by a switch operator, the other by an engineer. Those investigating the accident strove to relieve all parties of blame, or at least to minimize the damage to their reputations.

The company's main line from Montreal to Toronto followed a single track for much of its course, but west of Trenton the line divided into two sets of parallel tracks. The switching point was called Murray Hill, from a range of hills lying to the north. The site, roughly midway between Trenton and Brighton, had neither station nor village – just a signal and the box housing the switch operator.

As a rule, westbound express trains were switched onto the left-hand (south) track; the northern track was used by eastbound trains or slow westbound traffic that had been pulled aside to allow passage of faster expresses.

The signals posted were simple; a lamp showed a red light in one direction, a white light in the opposite direction. A Toronto-bound engineer facing a white light would know that the switch was open to the left-hand tracks, to which he had right of way. On the other hand, a red light would indicate that the switch was open to the right-hand tracks; he would have to halt until waved on.

Switching at Murray Hill was a memorable experience in itself. Westbound, the passage from single track to north track was fairly smooth, but passage to the south track was accompanied by a sharp jolt. Many people remarked that they could recognize the switch by that minor shock; even at night experienced travellers would know where they were when the train lurched over that switch to the southern rails.

In the early hours of November 15, 1898, the switch and signal were being operated by John Murphy, a Grand Trunk employee of six years' standing. He had been on duty since 7:00 p.m. – 12-hour shifts were the rule. At 1:52 a.m. a freight approached from the east. He directed it onto the south track, then reset the switch. The next westbound train to come up would be facing a red light, which would also indicate that the way was open to the north track. Eastbound trains on the north track would be facing a white signal light.

About 4:45 a.m. an eastbound freight, No. 96, chugged along the northern tracks towards Murray Hill junction. Thomas Ivens of Toronto was engineer; strung out behind were 24 loaded boxcars. Ivens was about 1.5 miles (2.5 kilometres) from the switch. He could not see what colour of signal was turned in his direction but he knew he should slow down; even if he was cleared to run on he would have to cross the switch at a fairly low speed.

The first mistake had been made by switchman John Murphy. The timetable and messages available to him would have indicated that a westbound express was due, yet he had left the switch set to allow westbound access to the northern tracks. Even so, that should not have been fatal. The Montreal-Toronto express was still facing a red light and must stop.

Enter the Grand Trunk's No. 5 express. It had left the Trenton station, struggled up a steep grade, and was now rushing westward down the slope towards the switch at about 50 miles per hour (80 km/hr). In the locomotive cab were William Brady (engineer) and John Macdonald (fireman), both of Belleville. Brady was considered to be an excellent employee, who had patented some improvements to locomotives. He was fully rested, having just come off a 16-hour break.

And yet, inexplicably, the No. 5 did not slow down as it approached Murray Hill. Brady seemed oblivious to the red light facing his train. The locomotive thundered by the switchbox, passing onto the north track and proceeding on a collision course with the No. 96 freight.

Brady had not only run through a red signal; he had missed another warning as well. There would have been no bumping jerk at the switch, the jolt that characterized passage to the south track. Had he looked from his cab, the engineer would have realized that there were rails to his *left* when there should have been tracks on his *right*. Still he went on, closing rapidly on the slow-moving freight.

Ivens and his fireman were the first to recognize the danger. They set their own brakes, then leaped to safety. Moments before the crash, William Brady realized his error and braked as well. It was too late. The No. 5 struck the No. 96 with such force that the locomotive cabs were flattened; the engines wound up boiler-to-boiler. Brady and Macdonald, the only men who could have explained the oversight, were killed instantly.

The freight with its many cars was like a hammer; two inertia-driven Pullman sleepers at the end of the express served as an anvil. The baggage/express car completely telescoped the following second-class coach and penetrated six feet (two metres) into a first-class

**Murray Hill
September 15, 1898**

No. 96 freight   IMPACT   Murray Hill   No. 5 express   Trenton

← To Toronto   To Montreal →

No. 5 express should have taken south track but was switched on to north track, ignoring a red signal in the process.

coach. The express car did great damage, yet sustained little itself. The Toronto *Globe* reported:

> Mr. C.W. Winter, a messenger of the Canadian Express Company, was in his car just behind the tender of the express train, and he was thrown almost from one end of the car to the other, but even then did not think the accident a serious one. He concluded that the engine had struck a cow and began to gather up hot coals from his stove which had been scattered over the floor of the car by the force of the collision, and while still engaged in this he was told of the serious nature of the accident by the trainmen who came to the door of his car to see if he was killed.

The same newspaper pieced together a vivid account of events following the crash. It shows something of the journalistic standards of 1898, and if the reader finds it rather lurid, it is actually subdued and tasteful when compared to accounts of wrecks in 1854, 1857 and 1864:

> It was intensely dark, and the shrieks of the injured rose above the hiss of the steam escaping from the broken pipes. The baggage car and the second-class coach were an indistinguishable mass and when the trainmen hurried with their lanterns to the heap of wreckage they found blood trickling from the floor of the second-class coach and falling on the rails beneath.

Passengers had dismounted from other cars and the work of rescue began. The *Globe*'s narrative continued:

> Conductor Robert Purdon sent men in each direction for help, and passengers and employees on the road worked together drag-

ging away timbers and twisted iron, taking out the dead and injured alike. The first to be picked up were three Russian immigrants, all dead, and it was two hours later and broad daylight before the last wounded was taken away…. Help came from many quarters…. Farmers living half a mile away, who were awakened by the crash, came hurrying over the fields with lights and valuable assistance to the train hands.

In ramming its way through the coach, the baggage car had tilted upwards and to one side, its floor slicing through roughly 12-18 inches (26-39 cm) above the floor of the coach. To that extent it differed from the Wanstead wreck of 1902, where a telescoping express car struck higher up and exacted a ghastly toll. As it was, 11 people died and 14 were seriously injured. One second-class traveller was hurled through three partitions, ended up in the following first-class coach, and walked away. His seatmate was killed.

The casualties were a mixed lot. They comprised two trainmen (Brady and Macdonald), an off-duty engineer travelling in the stricken coach, two Toronto cattle dealers and six German-speaking immigrants from Russia – four of them members of one family (father, mother, two daughters). One of the Toronto men had been carrying between $600 and $900. Little of the money was found; it was speculated that a ghoulish thief had robbed the body.

A coroner's inquest was convened with 24 jurors. Cross-examination of Murphy, the switchman, was particularly harsh; it was implied that his oversight in leaving the switch open to the north track had caused the accident. However, the most obvious and direct factor was engineer Brady's running through a red signal onto the wrong track.

Throughout the inquest a series of witnesses tried to lift the blame from Murphy and Brady. Particular attention was paid to salvaging the reputation of the dead engineer. At least two witnesses, including Ivens, the freight engineer, suggested that a steam valve may have burst in the No. 5's cab, creating a distraction and obscuring vision. The only problem with this theory was that not a shred of evidence could be produced to support it.

On November 17 the inquest jury brought in its findings. It stated flatly that the tragedy was due entirely to Brady's running through a red signal and continuing down the wrong track. Having fixed the blame, the jury added that Brady was "as faithful and trustworthy a driver as was in the service of the company" – in spite of the negligence just proven. The jury declared that Brady had *not* been overworked and that the existing switch was a satisfactory device. That let the Grand Trunk off the hook. The jurors further praised Murphy for his years of accident-free service. The verdict made for curious reading – by turns blunt and evasive, humane and forgiving. Ever aware of human fallibility, the jurors condemned negligence, but heaped praise upon the men whose carelessness had killed 11 people.

WANSTEAD, Ontario

DECEMBER 26, 1902

Most Canadian railway disasters were caused either by mechanical or metallurgical failure or by human error on the part of train crews. Two major wrecks stand out for having resulted from mistakes made by despatching personnel. At Wanstead, Ontario (December 26, 1902) and Canoe River, British Columbia (November 21, 1950), trains running according to orders in crew hands collided head-on with devastating results. The Wanstead tragedy was particularly dramatic and poignant; the despatchers involved realized their error almost as soon as it was made, and spent ten minutes trying to avert the calamity they foresaw.

Wanstead itself was a village of some 200 people situated 42 miles (65 kilometres) west of London, on the busy Grand Trunk line that connected Toronto and Hamilton with Sarnia, Windsor and American border cities. Although a small community, Wanstead had a lengthy siding, almost one mile (1.6 kilometres) long, with the station roughly midway between the east and west switches. Since traffic stopped here infrequently, the station and telegraph office were not manned at night.

Much of the line was controlled by despatcher James G. Kerr in London. On the night in question he was concerned with several trains, notably a westbound passenger train – the No. 5 "Pacific Express" – and an eastbound freight. Kerr was having difficulty arranging a "meet," where one train would take to a siding while the other passed through on the main line. He was especially concerned about unnecessary delay of the No. 5, which was carrying district supervisor W.E. Costello, who might demand explanations if the express was held up without good cause. As it was, the No. 5 was already running an hour late, due partly to heavy Christmas holiday traffic and partly to a snowstorm that was howling across southwestern Ontario.

The storm affected other people's thinking as well. When supervisor Costello approached Tom MacKenzie, engineer of the "Pacific Express," asking if he could ride in the locomotive cab, he was told that his presence would constitute an unnecessary distraction when the crew had to be especially vigilant. Costello saw the wisdom of this and chose instead to travel in a Pullman coach.

Despatcher Kerr had originally intended to have the two trains meet at Wyoming, a small town along the route, but the late-running No. 5 made this impractical. He sent a message cancelling the Wyoming rendezvous order. At 9:48 p.m. Kerr sent Telegraph Train Order 931 from his London post to the station agents at Wyoming and Watford, 12 miles (19 kilometres) apart. It read, "No. 5 Eng.980 and extra East Eng.773 will meet at Wanstead." This order was to be handed to the engineer and conductor of both trains. At Wyoming the freight crew received their instructions. A telegraph message back to London acknowledged that the orders had been delivered and were understood. After that, things began to unravel.

Kerr used the telegraph to issue orders; that ensured instructions and acknowledgements would be in writing. He also used it casually to keep informed of train movements. Having issued Order 931, he began to wonder about its wisdom. The freight was to proceed from Wyoming to Wanstead and take the siding before the express could be released from Watford. However, the freight was delayed. Kerr asked the Wyoming station agent why this was so; the agent replied that he would find out.

While waiting for information on the freight, Kerr contacted the Watford station agent, Andrew Carson, a 35-year veteran of Grand Trunk service. Precisely what was communicated would later be disputed. According to Kerr, the telegraphic chatter was about the *possibility* that Order 931 might be cancelled. Carson would claim that Kerr clearly signalled, "Bust [cancel] the order."

It was 9:57 p.m. At this point, John McAuliffe, conductor of the "Pacific Express," entered the Watford station to check for orders. His train was facing a "board" or stop signal. When he asked for instructions, agent Carson replied, "I had an order for you, but it has been 'busted.'" McAuliffe then asked for a clearance from Watford; Carson gave it immediately. Just before 10:00 p.m. the "Pacific Express" pulled out. So far as its crew was concerned, they had a clear run through to Wyoming unless stopped earlier by signals.

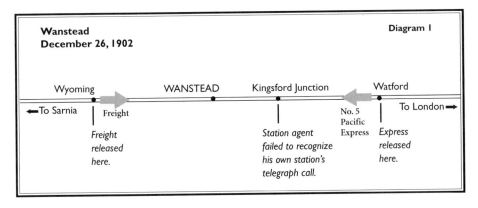

Wanstead
December 26, 1902

Diagram 1

Wyoming   WANSTEAD   Kingsford Junction   Watford

←To Sarnia   Freight   No. 5   To London ➡

Freight   *Station agent*   Pacific   *Express*
released   *failed to recognize*   Express   *released*
here.   *his own station's*   *here.*
                              telegraph call.

In releasing the express, Carson had ignored a basic company rule – that an explicit telegraphed order could be cancelled only by *another* explicit telegraphed order. Later he would claim that in practice several train orders had been annulled informally using the term "Bust it." Kerr would vehemently deny that such a thing was ever done. Even if he was correct, Kerr was probably guilty of confusing agents with his frequent calls and tendency to communicate *thoughts* as well as specific instructions. His status also intimidated Carson, who did not question the acts or judgement of one he deemed his superior.

While Carson and McAuliffe were conferring at Watford, Kerr was again wiring the Wyoming agent, asking if the freight would soon be moving. The agent replied that it was ready to leave, then asked, "Will I stop it?"

"Let it go," replied Kerr.

At this point Kerr realized that he had still not received confirmation that No. 5's crew had been given their copy of Order 931. He rang up Watford once more – it was 10:00 p.m. – to be informed that the express had just left. A half-minute was lost in recriminations between the London despatcher and the Watford agent. Then Kerr telegraphed Wyoming, trying to halt the freight. It was already pulling out and gathering speed. The agent dashed to the platform to flag it down with a lantern.

Aboard the freight a rear brakeman spotted the dim lantern amid the snowstorm and suspected that somebody, perhaps the conductor, had been left behind. He signalled for a stop. Conductor J.A. Graham, anticipating the brakeman's belief, signalled back, showing that he was aboard. The freight crew settled back for the ten-minute run to Wanstead.

In the London despatching centre, James Kerr realized he must halt the "Pacific Express" before it reached Wanstead's western switch. He began ringing Wanstead station on the offchance that the agent might have come back to the office for something; he could flag the express at the eastern switch. However, Kerr's best hope lay two miles (three kilometres) east of Wanstead, at Kingsford Junction, a small station equipped with a sema-phore. He tried wiring the post to have a "Stop" signal hoisted. There was no response. Kerr was going frantic. Was the Kingsford Junction agent absent? Was he asleep?

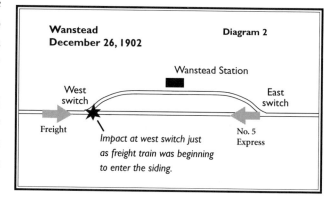

He was not. Seventeen-year-old James Troyer was on duty, diligently studying railway timetables. This was only his third day and first night on the job. Troyer had had little more than ru-dimentary telegraphy instruction. His machine had been clacking ceaselessly for the last two minutes as Kerr communicated with Watford and Wyoming stations. Now, when his attention was demanded, the youth did not recognize his own station call. Seven or eight minutes passed before he acknowledged his presence. Despatcher Kerr urged him to stop the express. Already it was too late; the train was even then rumbling through at 50 miles per hour (80 km/hr). It was 10:08 p.m.

There remained one hope that a collision might be averted – if the freight reached Wanstead siding before the No. 5. Indeed, that nearly happened. As it slowed for the approach, brakeman James Smith jumped from the train and ran ahead, intending to open the west switch so that the freight could roll onto the siding in one uninterrupted movement. On this night, however, heavy snow impeded Smith, and when he reached the switch he found it frozen. The freight rolled half-a-car length past the switch, still on the main line. It was backed up again and Smith wrestled the switch open. However, two minutes had been lost. Just as the freight locomotive began moving forward again, at the very point of entering the siding, the "Pacific Express" came rushing down at full speed. Brakeman Smith tried vainly to flag it down. It was 10:10 p.m. and time had run out.

In the last few seconds before the collision the freight conductor and fireman jumped clear. Aboard the express, engineer MacKenzie had barely discerned the freight's headlamp in the snow but had believed that the locomotive was on the siding. When he realized the true situation the time was past for braking. The great Mogul locomotive bowled the smaller freight engine off the tracks and was itself flipped over on its back. Two railroaders died instantly – James Gillies (the freight engineer) and A. Ricketts (fireman aboard the express).

The impact wrought strange consequences. At either end of the accident – the freight caboose, the No. 5's sleeping cars – people felt a bump rather than a crash. It was in the forward part of the express that the Wanstead collision became a nightmare of death and suffering.

LADIES' FURS
SABLE RUFFS,
SABLE RUFFS,
TIPPED FOX RUFFS,
TIPPED FOX SCARFS,
SABLE FOX RUFFS,
SABLE FOX RUFFS,
SABLE FOX RUFFS.
We keep nothing but the best, if you can rely on our goods.

**SPITTAL,
SABINE & CO.**

The Free Press·

TO-DAY'S WEATHER.
Fair and quiet cold

EVENING EDITION--SIXTEEN PAGES.

TO-MORROW'S WEATHER.
Continued Fair and Cold

4°
per annum allowed and separate, for to to Liverpool
THE
Canada
Compa
Managed by
HURON & ERIE

ONE CENT.   LONDON, ONT., SATURDAY, DECEMBER 27, 1902.   ONE CENT.

AWFUL RAILROAD WRECK ON GRAND TRUNK!
TWENTY-SEVEN KILLED; TWO SCORE INJURED

**Pacific Express Crashes Into a Freight at Wanstead, Forty Miles From this City, and Scene of Horror Follows---Day
Coaches Filled with Holiday Travellers, Telescoped by Two Baggage Cars and Passengers Piled in a Heap
Beneath the Wreckage...Dead and Dying, Women and Children and Men Pinned Down...Horrors
of Fire and of Ice-Cold Blizzard Add to the Awfulness of the Scene
---Cause of the Accident---Where the Blame Is Placed.**

LATER PARTICULAR

Immediately behind the engine/tender there had been a baggage car, and behind that a day coach with every seat taken. These two telescoped, with the floor of the baggage car slicing almost clear through the coach about level with the tops of the seats. Several passengers were decapitated. The lethal floor followed a strange course. It had tilted slightly to one side, so that all fatalities were on one side of the coach. People sitting in one seat were spared while neighbours in front or beside them perished. Some regained consciousness to find themselves pinned between seats and the baggage car floor. Pure luck had helped baggageman Alexander Caulfield. He had been sitting in his car, reading a newspaper, when the crash occurred. A reporter wrote, "He was carried with the car in its awful furrowing of the day coach. He received painful but not serious injuries."

Back in London, despatcher Kerr had been waiting and hoping

Headlines from the London *Free Press*, December 27, 1902.

for a message to the effect that the freight had reached the Wanstead siding safely. When the telegraph sprang to life it was supervisor Costello reporting the wreck and asking for auxiliary trains to be sent. Emergency action followed. From Sarnia and London went trains with wrecking equipment, extra coaches and medical personnel.

At the crash site, one threat, fire, surfaced and was quickly snuffed out by people throwing snow on the few small flames that appeared. Honours for preventing a conflagration were evenly divided between conductor McAuliffe and a passenger, A.C. Clarke of Sarnia; the former retrieved fire extinguishers from the two Pullman sleepers, then turned these cars into first aid stations. Two doctors and three nurses who had been among the passengers gave what help they could.

Extricating bodies and survivors was time-consuming. Up to two hours elapsed before some rescues were completed, during which time the injured endured cold and exposure. Not until the arrival of the auxiliary trains were jackscrews and wrecking bars available. The casualties were then lifted into coaches and taken directly to London, where hospital staff were waiting. Police kept the morbidly curious away from the mercy train, but a London *Advertiser* reporter managed to get aboard. He subsequently filed some of the most grimly lurid copy ever written about a Canadian train wreck.

The toll from this accident was 28 dead (two crewmen, 26 passengers) and 32 seriously injured. A coroner's inquest was convened and the full story was quickly told. A jury reported that the accident had been due to confusion regarding train orders; the crews were blameless, but Kerr and Carson were not. However, the jurors were unable to conclude which man was most responsible for the wreck. Given this uncertainty, the Attorney General of Ontario declined to lay charges against either employee.

There were numerous ironies about the Wanstead disaster. One victim, a 53-year-old travelling salesman, was discovered to have been a bigamist when two widows, one from Toronto, one from Hamilton, appeared to claim his body.

London's two newspapers, the *Free Press* (Conservative) and the *Advertiser* (Liberal), provided a study in contrasts in reporting the catastrophe. The former despatched a photographer to the crash scene, the latter an artist. Photo reproduction in journals was still unusual. The *Free Press* was reasonably subdued in its coverage, but *Advertiser* readers were treated to ghastly descriptions of the most gruesome scenes – the dismemberment of one victim, the trauma of another.

Both papers seized the opportunity to use the disaster as fodder in their own cross-town feud. The establishment of a new hospital had been a contentious issue some months before. When called upon to handle the emergency, London's recently-opened medical facilities proved excellent. The mayor, Adam Beck,* had supported the modernization programme, and the *Free Press* editorially congratulated him for his foresight. Having sniped at "carping critics" of the hospital, the paper added that "Mayor Beck was early in attendance" and concluded by declaring, "For being the pioneer of the great reform in this matter, Mayor Beck we doubt not will cheerfully bear all the blame for its excellent fruits."

The *Advertiser* was furious. In a short editorial entitled "SHAME," it condemned its rival for "loathsome lauding of Mayor Beck." The *Free Press* tut-tutted the *Advertiser* for intemperance. The *Advertiser* blasted its opponent as Beck's "pocket organ" which "uses this occasion to laud its idol in this indecent manner." Soon afterwards the two papers moved on to other disputes.

One cannot but shake one's head at the journalism of 95-odd years ago.

* Sir Adam Beck (1857-1925), "The Hydro Knight," promoted the use of public utilities to generate and distribute electric power in Ontario; in 1906, as Minister without Portfolio, he introduced the legislation creating the Hydro-Electric Power Commission of Ontario.

SAND POINT, Ontario

When the Canadian Pacific Railway's westbound No. 7 train departed Ottawa at 2:56 a.m. on February 9, 1904, its crew carried simple, specific written orders. Their express was to meet the eastbound No. 8 express at Sand Point, some six miles (ten kilometres) west of Arnprior. These instructions were known to engineer John Dudley, conductor J.T. Nidd and brakeman Alex Lamourie. The same orders had been passed to the crew of the No. 8 train.

When the No. 7 pulled into Arnprior the locomotive was giving trouble; Dudley was having difficulty maintaining steam pressure. That minor problem distracted the engineer. When he pulled out again, Dudley, a man with 21 years experience and an accident-free record, forgot his original orders. Instead of stopping at Sand Point where the "meet" was to take place, he ran straight through. When it became apparent that the express was going past the meeting point it became the duty of either Nidd or Lamourie to signal a halt. Unfortunately, Nidd had also forgotten the original orders, and the brakeman seems to have assumed that there had been a change of instructions. From the moment that the No. 7 hurtled past the Sand Point siding it was on a head-on collision course with the No. 8.

At the throttle of the eastbound train was 57-year-old Joseph Jackson, a respected 25-year veteran railroader. Some years earlier he had narrowly escaped death in an accident at Stittsville, just outside Ottawa. On that occasion he had remarked, "My next wreck will be my last – I won't come out of another wreck with the luck I had in this one." The words were prophetic.

About 2 miles (3 kilometres) west of Sand Point the CPR line followed a curve through brushland; the layout meant that approaching trains would not have a clear view of each other until one had rounded the curve. Forward visibility from a locomotive cab was seldom good anyway; today engineer Dudley was having special problems owing to frost on his

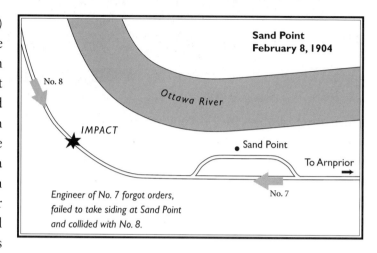

**Sand Point
February 8, 1904**

Ottawa River

No. 8

IMPACT

• Sand Point

To Arnprior →

No. 7

*Engineer of No. 7 forgot orders,
failed to take siding at Sand Point
and collided with No. 8.*

windows. His No. 7 was doing 30 miles per hour (50 km/hr) as it went through the curve and settled into the straight run.

Joseph Jackson evidently saw his nemesis bearing down. He hit the brakes, reversed his throttle and cut loose with his whistle. Every subsequent account of the accident paid tribute to the man who stayed at his post and died at the controls; he could have saved himself by jumping.

By odd coincidence the two locomotives that collided were virtual twins – Nos. 835 and 836 had been built in Scotland the previous year. They struck at 4:53 a.m. Curiously, nothing derailed; engines, tenders, and coaches all remained on the tracks. Nevertheless, the devastation was terrible. The Ottawa *Evening Journal* described it as follows: "In the force of the collision both locomotives were completely locked together, the baggage cars of each train telescoped with the tenders, nothing but the roofs remaining intact."

Two crewmen aboard the No. 8 were killed – engineer Jackson and an expressman. The principal carnage was in the No. 7, more particularly in the second-class coach filled with lumbermen. This

From the Ottawa *Citizen*, February 10, 1904.

THIRTEEN DEAD, 19 HURT SAND POINT COLLISION

East and West Bound Soo Expresses Meet in Head-On Collision—Engineer Jackson and Baggage-man Toole, of Ottawa, Killed.

Conductor James Nidd Admits His Train Ran Ahead of Orders Thereby Causing the Disaster—Scenes at the Wreck.

In a head-on collision between two C. P. R. passenger trains near Sand Point early yesterday morning, more than a dozen lives were lost and some nineteen people were injured more or less seriously. Traveling at a rapid rate of speed, the westbound Soo train—No. 7—in charge of Conductor Nidd, with Engineer Dudley, collided head-on with No. 8, the eastbound Soo train in charge of Conductor Forester and engineer Jackson. Failure of the up-going train to obey orders and remain on the siding at Sand Point till No. 8 passed, was the cause of the smash. An official list of the dead and injured follows:—

DEAD:

JOSEPH JACKSON, engineer, Ottawa.

W. McMULLEN, newsagent, Montreal.

ROBERT THOMPSON, express messenger, Montreal.

JOHN O'TOOLE, baggageman, Ottawa. Died at Union station.

JOSEPH CHALU, 89 Wall street, Hull.

DOLPHIS SEGUIN, 194 Brewery street, Hull.

J. CARRIERE, Ottawa. Address unknown.

M. LEBRAN, shantyman, Gaspe, Died in hospital.

ERNEST DUBOIS, Hochelaga, fireman. Died on train coming to Ottawa.

NELSON ROBERTSON, express messenger, Montreal.

WM. POULIOTTE, Whitney.

TWO UNIDENTIFIED.—

INJURED:

G. F. PRICE, fireman, Brockville, ser-

to Sand Point, the station agent there was called out of bed and a message was sent through to the divisional superintendent at Ottawa, Mr. H. B. Spencer. A special was quickly made up and accompanied by Trainmaster McCormick and Dr. Kidd, local physician of the company, the superintendent went up to the scene while auxiliaries with wrecking apparatus and crews were despatched from Carleton junction and other points. Doctors in Renfrew and Arnprior were also summoned while the company did everything to relieve the sufferings and secure the comfort of those figuring in the wreck.

It was a difficult job, however, to release many of those pinned under the wreck and that some of the injured survived under the circumstances is remarkable.

REMOVED TO COACHES.

As soon as the injured were got out they were looked after promptly and taken into the cars which remained on the track, where the doctors summoned to the scene dressed their wounds and put forth every effort to relieve their sufferings.

Afterwards a special ambulance train was made up and in colonist sleepers the injured were brought down to Ottawa, where they were assigned to the different hospitals. Some, however, were able to go home. News of the accident spread quickly around the city and at the C. P. R. a big crowd awaited the coming of the special. In the number were numerous city doctors and a good many friends and relatives of the train hands figuring in the fatality. There were some anxious faces for not until the train arrived was there any definite information respecting the extent of the fatality list or the exact condition of those who had been injured. The crowd surged up and down the platform and it was necessary for the station police to be augmented by members of the city force to keep back the eager

carriage telescoped the baggage car that had already telescoped the No. 7's tender.

Mail clerk Edwin Beach aboard the No. 7 had been working in the baggage car when the crash occurred. He woke up in a mass of debris that pinned him. He could feel another man, expressman Roy Thompson, trapped under him. Beach could even hear his companion's heart beating. Five hours passed before Beach was freed from the wreckage; in that time he listened as Thompson's heartbeat faded away.

Thirteen men died in the crash or within the next 36 hours; five of them were crewmen aboard the two trains. Rescue efforts were hampered by intense cold and a shortage of tools. Some victims died at the moment of being hauled free. It happened that one train was carrying a Catholic priest and the other had a Catholic bishop aboard; both men busied themselves with administering the last rites to some and tending shocked survivors.

A relief train made up in Arnprior rushed the 23-odd wounded to Ottawa, and a fleet of ambulances and horse-drawn cabs met them at the station. An inquest under coroner J.G. Cranston ruled on March 19 that the accident had been due entirely to negligence on the part of Dudley, Nidd and Lamourie, all of whom had readily admitted their lapses of duty. All the same, a sympathetic inquest jury sought to shift some of the responsibility to the impersonal corporation that employed the men; the verdict noted: "It is a hazardous thing on the part of the railroad to issue orders to train crews to take effect such long distances from the place of issuing as Sand Point from Ottawa, 57 miles."

The Sand Point wreck was one of the easiest of Canadian railway accidents to explain, being an obvious and admitted instance of human error.

AZILDA, Ontario

A feature of Canadian life from the late 1880s until the mid-1920s – from the opening of the prairies through to the mechanization of western agriculture – was an autumn migration of workers from east to west. These "harvest excursionists" descended by the thousands upon the wheatlands, toiling for three or four weeks before returning to homes in Ontario and points east.

On September 12, 1906, the CPR's No. 1 westbound, the "Imperial Limited," carried so many migrating harvesters that it was broken into three sections leaving Toronto at 1:45 a.m., 2:30 a.m. and 4:00 a.m. The third section included a heavily loaded baggage car and seven coaches. As usual, the lightly-built second-class or colonist cars followed the baggage car while a weighty Pullman sleeper brought up the rear.

Along the way the harvester train was to meet the eastbound No. 2 at Azilda, a small town 7 miles (11 kilometres) west of Sudbury with a 2,500-foot (800-metre) siding. At 7:30 a.m. the harvest excursion train paused just short of the eastern switch, ready to take the siding once the late-running No. 2 arrived.

It was raining and the rails were slick. The No. 2, under the hand of engineer W. Thurlow, had managed to make up 11 minutes in the last 28 miles (47 kilome-

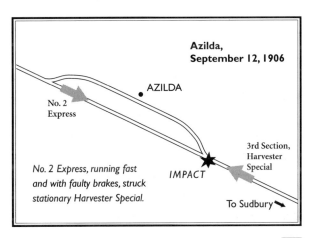

Azilda, September 12, 1906

AZILDA

No. 2 Express

3rd Section, Harvester Special

IMPACT

No. 2 Express, running fast and with faulty brakes, struck stationary Harvester Special.

To Sudbury

The locomotives head to head after the Azilda wreck, 1906. (National Archives of Canada PA29170)

tres). For a passenger train it had an unusual car in its makeup – a refrigerator car filled with salmon coupled between the tender and the baggage car. The brakes responded well enough on the eastward run, which sloped gently downhill. Three-quarters of a mile (1.2 kilometres) from the Azilda station, Thurlow reduced steam, and one-quarter of a mile (400 metres) off he applied brakes, intending to stop four car-lengths from the standing No. 1.

The gauges showed 70 pounds of pressure in the brake lines and 110 pounds in the reservoirs. In theory, everything should have worked, but on this day the No. 2 was in trouble. The brakes on the locomotive, tender, refrigerator car and baggage car came on, but nothing further aft was operating. The train scarcely slackened its pace, bearing down at 40 miles per hour (64 km/hr) on the harvester train.

Thurlow realized things were amiss. He signalled for emergency brakes, then blew off a steam signal to warn the crew of the "Imperial

Limited." However, there was no time for the other train to begin backing up. Both crews leaped to safety. With a great crash, the locomotive of the No. 2 ground its way into that of the harvester train.

The eastbound train's refrigerator car saved the passengers aboard; tons of salmon absorbed most of the force on that side, although the baggage car was smashed. The "Imperial Limited" had no such protection. Its baggage car directly telescoped the leading colonist car.

It was Wanstead all over again. The baggage car tilted and crashed through the coach, killing some and trapping others beneath its floor, which was loaded with trunks and other luggage. As at Wanstead, death struck capriciously, sparing some and snatching their neighbours. James W. Bartlet, a passenger in the stricken coach, described his own ordeal:

> I was three seats from the front of the car and I saw that ponderous baggage van come right into our car with hardly a moment's notice. I crouched down but two men who occupied the double seat with me were killed. I was pinned down for a few minutes, but releasing myself I crawled through a window, wondering at my escape. The baggage car just seemed to chew everything to pieces that was in its path.

Passengers alighting from the following coaches rushed forward to begin rescue efforts amid clouds of steam. The jumble of baggage had to be cleared away before they could reach travellers trapped between seats and under flooring. Some were imprisoned for more than two hours. Seriously injured cases were dashed to Sudbury. Over a three-day period reports of the toll fluctuated amid confusion over the identity of victims; a woman in Toronto received a telegram stating that her husband was dead; two hours later he telephoned to report himself safe and uninjured. It was finally established that 12 persons had died, including two girls aged 12 and 14 who were crushed between seats; their parents sitting immediately behind them escaped with minor injuries.

The immediate cause of the accident was clear – brake failure on the eastbound No. 2. But what had led to the brakes not functioning? That was the most important question raised in the investigations that followed. The possibility that the express might have been travelling too fast on wet rails, and that braking had been started too late, was scarcely weighed.

The answer to the stated question seemed to lie in two technical factors: the air brakes and the coupling system. Air brakes operate with key parts – the brake itself, a reservoir of pressurized air under each car, and the lines linking the reservoirs to the brakes. When an engineer applies brakes he opens a valve that releases air into the brake cylinder and slows the train. The same thing happens if part of a train uncouples; at the point where the cars break apart the brakes come on automatically.

However, an angle-cock valve in the system operates to override the air brakes for situations like yard shunting. If the valve is open, the air pressure in the system is controlled; if it is closed, the brakes aft of the valve do not work. An examination of the eastbound No. 2 disclosed that the angle cock valve on the rear of the baggage car was closed.

How it had come to be shut off was a mystery. It might have been closed manually, but such an error would have been unlikely; to do this a person would have had to crawl under the car and tamper with the device. There was no reason for any crewman to have done this at any stop between Sault Ste. Marie and Azilda.

The most likely culprits were two stay chains that were found dangling under the baggage car. Normally these would have been linked to the following car as a backup means of holding coaches together should a coupling fail. Was it possible that one or both chains had not been connected, or that they had come loose during travel? If so, could a swaying chain have struck the angle-cock valve on the brake mechanism and closed it? A crude test was conducted in which officials grabbed the chains and swung them about. It was found that the chains *could* touch the valve if they were swung violently. Never-

Crowds gather after the Azilda wreck, 1906 – in the background demolished rolling stock. (National Archives of Canada PA29168)

theless, it seemed improbable that ordinary train vibrations and rocking could have set the chains swinging with the force needed the reach the valve and bang it shut.

It should be remembered that the No. 2 had been running late and had been speeding to make up time. This may have caused the chains to loosen and swing violently; it would also mean that the train was moving faster than normal as it approached a braking situation. The coroner's inquest did not explore this factor. On September 19 the jury concluded that the accident was due to "a defective air brake service on No. 2 train, the defect being a closed angle cock on the rear of the mail car." There was no systematic probe to determine *how* it had been closed. The Azilda wreck was to be written off as a case of "mechanical failure" for which no person was to be blamed.

VANCOUVER, British Columbia

NOVEMBER 10, 1909

The city of Vancouver in 1909 was serviced by the British Columbia Electric Railway. Although it was primarily a passenger transit operation, with standard street cars, the firm also had electric locomotives which hauled and shunted freight cars.

At 5:10 a.m., November 10, 1909, electric locomotive No. 503 left the Carrall Street station, pulling a CPR flatcar, which was heavily loaded with timber, perhaps 27 tons of it. Most of this was 12 x 12-inch timber, more than 30 feet (9 metres) long. On top of these were four-inch planks. The car was so closely packed that a brakeman would have only 18 inches of working room between the load and his hand brake. The destination of the locomotive was an iron foundry on Nanaimo Road, where the flatcar was to be deposited on a siding.

Only three men worked the little train – David McDonough (engineer), Fred Wiggins (conductor) and William Burrows (brakeman). After some delays they reached the foundry, but discovered the switch to the siding was blocked by an empty CPR boxcar. Halting on the main BCER line, the crew applied the brakes on the flatcar, blocked the wheels with a cord of wood, then uncoupled the locomotive.

McDonough advanced to the eastern switch, backed onto the siding, and coupled onto the boxcar. He then backed further until he felt the thump of the boxcar nudging against the flatcar. Conductor Wiggins and brakeman Burrows peered down, their lanterns casting a dim glow. The boxcar was apparently well coupled to the flatcar. Burrows undid the brake; Wiggins removed the wooden cord block. The signal was given and McDonough began moving forward, towing both boxcar and flatcar onto the foundry siding.

According to the train crew, both cars moved ahead at least 6 feet (1.8 metres); at one time it was maintained that they advanced half a car length, indicating that the coupling was holding. Suddenly the flatcar separated from the boxcar and began rolling back.

Wiggins felt a jerk, knew that the flatcar was gone, and rushed to stop it. Seizing the wood block, he thrust it under the wheels of the car. Already, however, the flatcar had gathered too much momentum. It contemptuously bumped over the block and began rolling westward, down the BCER mainline.

Aboard the runaway car William Burrows tried to reset the brakes. Crowded by the lumber load, he could not get sufficient leverage to halt the monster. Burrows stayed with the car for about 150 feet (45 metres), then jumped. His haste in abandoning the car was understandable; further down the slope there was a trestle, and to jump there would have been suicidal. Engineer McDonough began backing down the track again, blowing his whistle to warn any traffic which might be in the way of the runaway car. It was a futile gesture.

At 5:50 a.m. a single tramcar of the BCER had let the Vancouver depot. Aboard were 24 people, most of whom were company employees bound for the New Westminster car shops. Just after 6:00 a.m. the tram passed the Lakeview station, virtually at the existing Vancouver city limits. The *Vancouver Daily Province* takes up the story:

It was dark at the time, and to make matters worse for the east-bound passenger car which had been following the freight car, the track curves between the point where the latter ran away, and the scene of the collision a quarter of a mile to the west. Owing to the darkness the motorman of the oncoming passenger car could not see the runaway freight rounding the curve, the headlight of the passenger car flashing off the track at a tangent, and not spotting the runaway as would have been the case had the track been perfectly straight.

Gathering speed during every foot of that fatal quarter-mile dash until its pace was terrific, the heavily loaded flatcar plunged into the oncoming passenger car a few hundred feet east of Lakeview station.... The crash of the collision, the impact of car against car, and the shriek of the dying and injured filled the air in an instant. The terrible din was heard several blocks, and then quiet suddenly followed, only to be broken in a moment by the renewed cries of the horribly maimed men who had lived through that awful 30 seconds.

As if they had been greased, the heavy timbers on the flatcar ... catapulted through the passenger coach, in a twinkling sweeping almost every vestige of the car body between the roof and the floor.

(Facing page) Coverage in the *Daily News-Advertiser* of the Vancouver disaster involving a runaway flatcar. (National Archives of Canada NL19360)

The Daily News-Advertiser.

FOURTEEN PAGES   VANCOUVER, BRITISH COLUMBIA. THURSDAY, NOVEMBER 11, 1909.   FIRST SECTION.

[PAR]LIAMENT [OP]ENS TO-DAY

—*—

of Speech From Throne — on Naval Policy Will be Deferred.

—*—

Own Correspondent.

November 10. — The [fr]om the Throne with which [ag]ency will open the session [gover]nent to-morrow afternoon [was] drafted at to-day's Cabi- [net]. Speculation as to its [...] as been freely going the [...] the Press for days past, [...]essentials of it have been [...]y foreshadowed. The prin- [...]re will be the reference to [...] programme which Parlia- [...]be asked to endorse. But [...] probably be no definite dis- [...] party attitude upon the [...]uring the debate on the Ad- [...] will probably be deferred [...] Naval Bill itself is intro- [...]

[...]the Government measures [...]e promised will be a Bill [...]th bookmaking and other [...]ace-track gambling; Bank- [...]nedment; the deferred In- [...]ill; amendments to the Im- [...]Act, and to the Law re- [...]ombines.

[...]ce will be made to His Ex- [...] Western tour, to the im- [...]In revenues, to the bounti- [...]t of this year and the gen- [...]erity of the country, [...]ow's proceedings will be [...]mal and ceremonial, as the [...] the Address will not be [...] until Friday. [...]ications point to an unusu- [...]attendance at the opening. [...]ph Smith and Mr. Martin [...] the only British Columbia [...]who have so far arrived to [...]n the session, but the mem- [...] the Prairie Provinces are [...]o in large numbers. [...] chief topics of political [...] the Naval Question and the [...]lumbia Elections, which are [...]n unusual amount of In-

Deep Distress in Two Cities

Due to Sad Calamity on Interurban Line Yesterday at Dawn— Timber Flat-car Breaks Loose from "Shunter" near Cedar Cottage and Crashes at Speed Into Early Morning Passenger- Car—Fourteen Occupants, Employees of Company and Other Workmen, Meet Terrible Death — Ten Remaining Gravely Injured—Fullest Investigation Being Instituted.

DEAD.

GEORGE THORBURN, married, B. C. Electric Railway motorman, 1110 Odlum Drive.
S. M. MITCHELL, widower, B. C. Electric Railway shops, 241 Keefer Street.
THOMAS TUTTLE, married and family, B. C. Electric Railway shops, 500 block Prior Street.
THOMAS BOWES, married and family, carpenter, 1549 William Street.
R. S. LYON, married and family, carpenter, 1607 Fourth Avenue East.
THOMAS FARMER, married, B. C. Electric Railway shops, Park Drive.
J. H. CROWTHER, Schaake Machine Works, New Westminster, 112 Sixth Avenue East.
WILLIAM JOHNSON, married and family, conductor, New Westminster.
T. E. HOLLAND, married and family, painter, B. C. Electric Railway shops, 1837 Keefer Street.
HARRY H. SLAYTON, married and family, Ross & Howard foundry, Waters Road, South Vancouver.
J. F. STEVENS, married, New Westminster Waterworks, Grove Crescent.
W. STEVENS, New Westminster Waterworks, Grove Crescent.
F. POCHIN, married and family, B. C. Electric Railway shops, 1852 Third Avenue East.
A. S. WILKINSON, married, B. C. Electric Railway shops, 1500 block Thirteenth Avenue.

INJURED.

WILLIAM HARRIS, conductor, Campbell Avenue; fractured arm and fractured skull; condition grave.
F. C. CARTY, Columbia Street, New Westminster, son of late Chief of Police Carty; compound fracture of skull; condition grave.
GEORGE CRAWFORD, 508 McMartin Street, New Westminster; internal abdominal injuries; condition grave.
W. P. HAINES, Burrard Hotel, City; scalp wound and pelvis crushed.
THOMAS B. JACKSON, employed at Fraser Hotel, New Westminster; ribs and chest injured; lives here with wife.
J. W. RUSHTON, 1005 Queen's Avenue, New Westminster; fracture of shoulder bones; serious; eldest son of J. B. Rushton, leader of the New Westminster Band; plays in Harpur's orchestra here.
ELI ZIMMERMAN, Central Park; scalp wounds and compound fracture, dislocation of ankle.
ROBERT FORSYTH, 731 Homer Street; scalp wounds and extensive contusions of chest and back.
CARL W. CARLSEN, 135 Hastings Street East; extensive scalp wounds.
J. D. TAYLOR, 999 Eighth Avenue; injured in chest.

In the darkness that came before | mission, and he has promised to lay | were detained by the police at the

CONSERVA[TIVE] OR LIB[ERAL]

—*—

Audience at Eburne [En]joyed Entertain[...]ing Performan[...]

Mr. F. G. T. Lucas w[...] champion of the Conserv[...] the Eburne meeting of [...] Liberals last night. Th[...] he was the only speake[...] form supporting the Pr[...] ernment, but at least hal[...] to judge from their atti[...] to be with him in the fi[...] good meeting from be[...] view, perhaps. At any r[...] attended, splendid atten[...] and the applause was [...] Messrs. J. W. Weart and [...]nell led off for the Liber[...] Mr. Lucas, with Messrs[...] Farris and F. C. Wade, [...] the finishing touches. [...] questioned the proposed [...] the old Court House, and [...] it ought to go into the [...] He contended also that [...] Government had hoarded [...] the expense of public w[...] Connell made the promi[...] Oliver were elected he [...] line through the Hope M[...] off—if not sooner. In [...] Court House Mr. Lucas [...] when the one one wa[...] Vancouver members pro[...] old one would remain in [...] of the Province, and that [...] for different action to b[...] be by the whole House [...] charge of hoarding, he [...] that whilst in 1903 and [...] $100,000 was spent in [...] last year the amount use[...] pose nearly reached the [...] dollar total. One spea[...] little was done in surve[...] lands, but he disposed of [...] ing that in the last year [...] been spent in survey [...] parties sent out. [...] Mr. Farris said that [...] should not guarantee the [...] C. N. R., but ought to [...]inion Government do mo[...] the Alberta Governmen[...]

Propelled by the terrific force, the timbers carried on through the passenger coach, mowing down every man in their path, and finally plunged to the ground at the rear end of the coach, besmeared with blood and bits of human flesh.

The roof of the car, broken and torn, but still holding together, fell like a pall over the jumbled mass of battered, slaughtered humanity that remained a quaking, shrieking jumble on the floor of the car next to its rear end.

Into this charnel house the first men to the rescue had to plunge in their search for the dead and the few who remained alive. Groping around in the darkness, sometimes lighted by the sickly rays of a few lanterns which had been secured, but more often guided by touch, the rescuers pulled body after body out of the wreck, a few living but the majority past human aid, though still warm and limp to the touch.

While this awful work was in process other men were pulling and pushing the fallen roof of the car clear of the floor in order that those bodies remaining beneath it might be secured as rapidly as possible. Suddenly the car roof was heaved over the side and down a 15-foot embankment and the magnitude of the disaster was laid bare – not a soul had escaped death or injury.

Fourteen men were killed on the spot, among them motorman George Thorburn. It is terrible to speculate on his last few conscious moments, alone at his post, as he saw the flatcar plunging towards his own tram. Conductor William Harris died on the 11th, raising the total to 15 dead. As the newspapers said, virtually every survivor suffered severe injuries.

A wrecking crew was on the scene within an hour. The tram car had been reduced to its truck frame and wheels; all else was debris.

The wreckers hauled the splintered wood to the side and burned it alongside the tracks. Later there was some criticism that possible evidence for an inquest had been destroyed. It is true that there was undue haste; the tracks were clear by 8:30 a.m. On the other hand, the most valuable item of material evidence had been preserved – the runaway flatcar itself.

A coroner's inquest was convened on the day of the accident. There were several adjournments, and the inquiry was not concluded until December 4 after nine sessions and 40 witnesses. Virtually the whole of the inquest was devoted to studying the situation at the iron foundry switch, where the coupling between the flatcar and the boxcar had failed.

Or had it failed? Had the two cars been properly coupled in the first place? Within hours of the accident two city detectives had looked at the couplings and declared them to be in good order. "It looks like the cars were not coupled at all," their report stated.

The items in question were regular M.C.B. couplings, standard railway equipment, designed to couple automatically. A brakeman, operating a mechanism on the cars, opened the couplings; on impact they closed and locked as pins fell into place. In theory they could not come apart once the linkage had been made; forward movement would prove that a reliable coupling had been made. Moreover, the freight crewmen maintained throughout that the whole train had advanced a few feet before the flatcar broke loose.

Their statement about the couplings having been secure enough for the flatcar to have advanced a few feet was repeatedly challenged; the fact that the car had run away seemed proof to many witnesses that the connection had not been properly made.

Nevertheless, towards the end of the hearings several other witnesses reported other instances of "automatic" couplings that had not held. Thomas Coughlin, a CPR freight conductor, testified of several instances where apparently well-secured couplings had failed. The reasons for such failures had varied – pins not dropping all the way into place in which case an unusually heavy jerk might release the couplings, unusual strains on drawbars, uneven tracks, and worn knuckles on the couplings themselves which resulted in some unexpected incidents on curves. George McArthur, a Vancouver brakeman, testified that over eight years he knew of several instances of couplings failing. As recently as November 22, when the inquest was still sitting, another unexplained coupling failure had occurred in Vancouver.

On December 4 the coroner and his jury met with other witnesses at a BCER siding where the boxcar and flatcar were sitting. The two cars were repeatedly coupled and the couplings tested. They worked perfectly. There seemed to be no unusual wear on them. None of the reasons advanced for spontaneous uncouplings seemed to apply in this particular instance.

That evening the jury retired to consider the evidence. Not everyone was convinced that the freight crew had checked the couplings sufficiently, Moveover, there was some criticism about their having uncoupled the flatcar on the main line in the first instance. The only thing that seemed to be generally agreed upon was that the excessive loading on the flatcar had left insufficient space for the brakeman to operate.

After two hours the jury returned. They were critical of several minor items, notably the lack of a public city morgue to permit more orderly identification of victims in such disasters. Yet as to the reasons for the accident itself, the jurors were singularly mute. The nub of their conclusions was wrapped up in an evasive statement:

We find no evidence to show that there was any criminal negligence on the part of the crew in charge of the freight train, nor have we found that the crew have disobeyed any rules in connection with the performance of their duties on the morning of the accident.

The causes of the accident remained as obscure as when the inquest began. Had the flatcar been securely coupled to the boxcar? If so, why had the coupling parted? No satisfactory conclusion was ever published.

NEW WESTMINSTER, British Columbia

NOVEMBER 28, 1909

The crash near Vancouver's Lakeview station was still in the public mind – the coroner's inquest was still going on – when another railway catastrophe occurred. This one, however, excited much less attention in the press. The reason was that the victims were all members of a community that was the object of recurring suspicion and hostility – Japanese workmen.

It had been raining for two days in Vancouver, and on Saturday, November 27, the rain became a drenching downpour, the heaviest in memory. Creeks filled and swelled; where a trickle might normally be found, a torrent now appeared. Throughout British Columbia there were washouts and mud slides affecting both road and rail traffic.

In the early hours of Sunday, November 28, word spread through the work camps of the Great Northern Railway that a gang was to go out to check and repair road beds. One group, headed by a man called Ito, was designated for this task. On this occasion, however, Ito had trouble rounding up his men. Some could not be found; others refused to venture out in such miserable weather. Another foreman, K. Katsuta, had more luck in assembling his men, and eventually his group was assigned to the work train.

The train left Vancouver at about 6:00 a.m., heading eastward. There were 43 people aboard. The engineer was one Beattinger (not further identified in press reports), and there were three other trainmen aboard. There was also an unauthorized passenger, G.W. Kent, a commercial traveller who was bound for Cloverdale on a vacation. He was allowed by the engineer to ride in the locomotive. All the other 38 men were members of Katsuta's work gang.

The locomotive was pulling its tender, a boxcar which held the workmen, three flatcars and a caboose. The workmen were huddled near the rear of their boxcar, trying to sleep while keeping each other warm and dry. The rain was still falling as the train grumbled along at about 20 miles per hour.

Engineer Beattinger peered ahead, but visibility was poor. The headlight was very weak, and the best that could be seen was the reflection of the light thrown back by the glistening rails. At 6:09 a.m. the train was starting to cross Kilby Creek, one mile (1.6 kilometres) west of New Westminster's city limits.

Kilby Creek, a tributary of the Brunette River, was serviced by a 6-foot (2-metre) culvert pipe, covered by an embankment of coarse, grey sand. The embankment was some 20 feet (6 metres) high and ran a length of 500 or 600 yards (450-550 metres). Once across the creek valley, the train would enter a cut, itself formed some eight years before by removal of the sand for the embankment.

Normally the creek would have been a gently flowing stream, but during the night it had swollen to the lip of its banks, tearing out tree stumps and undermining boulders. Debris swept up by the rampaging waters had been carried downstream, lodging firmly in the culvert. A small lake had formed behind the "fill" which had become a dam, and then the water soaked through, weakening the embankment. A track-walker might have spotted this dangerous situation, but no such inspection had been carried out for at least 12 hours.

The locomotive steamed along the tracks; everything seemed to be holding well. It was almost across Kilby Creek when a huge hole yawned open in the fill. The tender went down into it, followed by the boxcar. The latter went halfway down; the other half protruded from the hole where it was hit by the adjacent flatcar, which sliced through it – and its occupants – like a huge knife. The other two flatcars, jammed together and derailed, stopped at the edge of the hole. The caboose never left the tracks.

In the locomotive, the engineer and fireman had jumped as soon as they felt the tracks slipping away behind them, drawing the engine back. Beattinger was badly injured and would spend several weeks in hospital. Kent, the hitchhiking commercial traveller, had one foot nearly severed in the crash, and later in hospital it would be amputated.

One of the Japanese survivors declared that it had been like falling in a dream, followed by the impact and unconsciousness. One Miyoruma found himself pinned in the boggy sand with his head under water. He dragged himself clear, only to find that he had two broken legs.

Rescue efforts were hampered by the darkness, continuing rain, the steep banks of the ravine, and the torrent of water which continued to pour through Kilby Creek. The Europeans present testified later that the Japanese workmen were stoical, dignified and brave; there were no screams, no hysteria, just a few groans while the living did their best to retrieve the dead.

The Daily News-Advertiser.

ELVE PAGES   VANCOUVER, BRITISH COLUMBIA. TUESDAY, NOVEMBER 30, 1909.   TWELVE PAGES

ONNEL OF AL COURT

cdonald, Chief Justice—
rving and Martin, and
W. A. Galliher,

ember 29.—The British
rt of Appeals was to-day
follows:
Macdonald, of Rossland,
al Leader, to be Chief
Justice Irving, and Jus-
and Mr. W. A. Galliher.

ancies in the Supreme
l F. B. Gregory, of Vic-
Dennis Murphy, of Ash-
ointed.

nter Hurricane.

P. R., November 27.—
se barque Navaganto
ere with her mainmast
erwise damaged. She
arbadoes on November
cargo of molasses for
deira. On November
ntered the West Indian
l sprung a leak. The
no chart of the place,
close until he saw the
en the Revenue cutter
nt to the rescue. The
er, needed only guid-
ered port unassisted.

E HAS OLLAPSED

inster Under Pressure
Front of Building
ropped Up.

estminster the floods
a considerable amount
he streets sloping down
These were all out or

THREE DAYS' RAINSTORM

Demoralises Traffic and General Communication Conditions in and
Round This City.

PRECIPITATION WAS
QUITE PHENOMENAL

Only Rough Estimates of Damage Yet
Obtainable—Island and Lower
Mainland Both Suffer.

After one of the worst rainstorms
ever experienced on the Coast of British
Columbia, there comes a long tale of
damaged roads, flooded cellars and
basements, water supplies disrupted
and many tales of disaster. From all
parts the story is the same, and as the
floods abate and communication be-
comes easier, the list of trouble grows
longer and larger. Vancouver itself
had a washing such as she has never
had before. For 48 hours, with only
a small interval, the rain fell. It fell
in sheets and instead of relaxing it
only seemed to fall the heavier as the
hours passed on. It is estimated that
some seven and a-half inches fell during the two days from Saturday at
noon to yesterday at the same hour.
The rainfall on Sunday was at the rate
of a quarter of an inch per hour, a
phenomenal downpour. Technically,
the rain fell uniformly, and was due
to a conglomeration of circumstances.
The air was charged with moisture,
and a continually shifting wind causing a constant change of temperature
brought about the downpour. The
barometer was fairly high throughout
the storm, but as soon as the weather
showed signs of clearing it fell.
Of the damage perhaps the most
serious, locally, was the

WASH-OUT ON BROADWAY,

near Heather Street, where the road
was completely destroyed for the
length of the crossing. There was
a second serious washout on the
same street at the Bridge Street
crossing. The same scene was
re-enacted there and a raging
torrent carried away the whole of
the roadbed. It was of course im-

level. In this latter district, floods
are not unusual, and when the rain
began, flooding was expected, but the
inundation passed expectation.
In Mount Pleasant the damage to
cellars was also heavy. The printing
office owned by Mr. A. H. Timms, on
Fourteenth Avenue, near Westminster
Avenue, presented the appearance of
an island, the only means of access
being over planks laid from the road,
which is considerably above the level
of the houses on that street. A house
next door to the printing works on
Fourteenth Avenue was flooded on
Saturday night, and the owner had to
take out his wife and children on
horseback. A barn at the rear of this
house, which contained oats, had its
contents swept away. All the cars
from the barns at the corner of Fourteenth Avenue and Westminster Avenue had to be removed on Saturday
night, as it was feared that, owing
to the rush of water underneath, the
foundations of the building were unsafe.
But these are only a few instances
of the effects of the rain. Practically every house with a cellar can tell
the same story. Of the damage done
in the

CENTRAL PARTS OF THE CITY

that suffered, the Brunswick Pool
Rooms was perhaps the most severe.
The place was flooded, and it is estimated that some $4,000 will be re-
quired to repair the building. Two or
three feet of water in the basement of
the First Presbyterian Church prevented the congregation from holding
service there on Sunday morning,
while the Sunday School class in the
afternoon was also postponed. Fortunately the firemen arrived in the
afternoon and the furnace was set to
work about 4 o'clock, and the evening
service was held as usual. Damages
are reported to be trifling. Across
the way, at the Salvation Army Hotel
Welcome, however, affairs were of a
more serious nature. The basement
was flooded with two feet of water
and a quantity of clothing, some be-
longing to the Army and some to the
lodgers, was practically ruined. Down
at the Woods Hotel, where there is
only a small four inch drain which allowed the water practically free play,
damages are estimated at over $1,000.
It was stated that the communication with

CENTRAL PARK

had been affected. This is not true.
For some time the B. C. E. R. has
been running only one track, owing to
the grading on Hastings Street, and

TWENTY-THREE JAPANESE DEAD

As Result of Washout on G. N. R.
Near Sapperton—Tragic Scene in
Grey Dawn.

CULVERT GAVE WAY
UNDER WORK-TRAIN.

Several White Men Injured—Heroism
of the Japanese Sufferers—
Wounded Recovering.

By far the worst of the disasters
from the recent heavy rains, was a
railway wreck on the Great Northern
Railway near Sapperton on Sunday,
when 23 Japanese workmen were
killed and 14 injured. Early on Sunday morning a work-train had started
out from Vancouver to do some repairs on the road. Engineer Beat-
tiger and Fireman Purdy were on the
engine, and in the boxcar behind were
about 40 Japanese, and three white
men were in the caboose. All went
well till they were nearing Sapperton, at about 6:30 a. m.. It was still
quite dark, and as the train dashed
along it was impossible for the engineer to see that the supporting earth
had washed out under an embankment over the culvert which carried
Kilby Creek under the track. The
speed of the engine carried it safely
over the washout, but the track sagged under the tender, and it slid
down, carrying the engine back.
The red boxcar in which the Japanese were riding following the tender, plunging headlong into the hole
in such a manner that half of it
stood in the air above the level of the
tracks. The first flatcar following

CUT THE BOXCAR IN HALF.

The two other flatcars piled on each
other on top of the hole, and the unfortunate Japanese were crushed and
killed in the falling debris. The caboose, in which were Ellis, the conductor, the timekeeper and a brakes-
man, never left the tracks, and its occupants were quite uninjured.
The engineer and fireman jumped
when they felt the engine falling, and,
strange to say, escaped from the

VERY CURI COINCID

Victor Johndro Falls Six
Dominion Trust Compa
at New Westmins

An accident similar to
occurred here recently,
fell from the Dominion
pany's building for a dis
storeys, occurred last ni
Westminster. Strange to
accident took place from th
pany's building, but inste
ten storeys, the man call
Victor Johndro is the
man who fell, and he is
Royal Columbian Hospital
ken leg, and suffering fro
of bruises. He is gone
however. Johndro is a
member of the Sixth Regi
first-class rifle shot.
It appears that Johndro
on the fifth storey, went
in his sleep, and climbed
trap door at the top of the
to the roof. He then walk
the air-shaft, and after
storeys came in contact w
roof through which he pa
ing comparatively gently
below.

IN THE CAU OF CHA

Relief Committee Has
Sum to Distribute Amo
urban Accident Suff

The handsome sum of $1
realised at the benefit con
originated with Mr. Con
was held at the Opera Hous
ing, and of which a detaile
tion appears in the "
Drama" columns.
The Mayor, as secretary
lief Committee, announce
audience the amount that

Twenty-two workmen, including foreman Katsuta, had been killed in the crash. The injured had to wait almost two hours before a relief train arrived. Very few personal accounts of the wreck were subsequently published; newspaper editors apparently made no effort to bridge the language gap with the survivors. Moreover, the gathering of funds to help those left (including at least eight widows and several children) fell mainly to the Japanese community, with little aid from European citizens. There were not even any telegrams of condolences from dignitaries.

A coroner's inquest opened on December 7, and proceeded slowly, with several adjournments, until the 17th. Despite its duration, it appears to have been a perfunctory affair, as perhaps was inevitable when the cause of the accident was so clearly due to the freak storm which had been in progress at the time. Nevertheless a contractor, C.T.W. Piper, was critical of the culvert and fill in a place where a proper bridge would have been more appropriate. Piper descried the system present at the time as "one of the most disgraceful pieces of work ever tolerated." Shortly after the accident he had heard that the culvert had included an internal brace which might have acted to trap debris and thus block the flow of water. On examining the culvert he had found *four* such braces. The culvert blockage had been virtually inevitable in these circumstances. Railway lawyers cross-examined Piper with such ferocity that the jurors demanded the bullying cease.

The inquest results were a foregone conclusion. On the 17th the jurors reported back, exonerating the freight crew and attributing the accident to the storm. Their sole recommendation of substance was that a night track-walker be employed during severe rainstorms.

(Facing page) Headlines in the *News-Advertiser* record the New Westminster disaster as well as the torrential rains that led to it. (National Archives of Canada NL19359)

SPANISH RIVER, Ontario

JANUARY 21, 1910

Twenty-seven miles (40 kilometres) west of Sudbury, near Webbwood, Ontario, occurred Canada's fourth-ranking train disaster. It was a grim event, involving death by impact, fire and drowning. It resembled the Desjardins Canal wreck of 1857 in that it was rooted in metal fatigue close to a bridge.

In the early afternoon of January 21, 1910, the CPR's No. 7 train was westbound at full speed, running from Montreal to Minneapolis. It had left Sudbury at noon with about 100 passengers aboard, stopped briefly at Nairn Centre, and left there at 12:42 p.m. The No. 7 consisted of the locomotive and tender, a mail and baggage car, an express car, two second-class coaches (variously termed colonist or immigrant cars), a first-class coach, a diner and a Pullman sleeper.

The immigrant cars were fitted with stoves, and several passengers had gathered around these, waiting to prepare their own meals. First-class passengers were beginning to gather in the diner; most people in that car were near the front.

It was about 12:55 as the train approached the Spanish River on a gently-sloping grade. The river was about 250 feet (80 metres) wide and 30 feet (9 metres) deep; it was frozen at this date. A high cantilever bridge carried the line across the

Map from the *Evening Telegram*'s coverage of the Spanish Rives disaster.

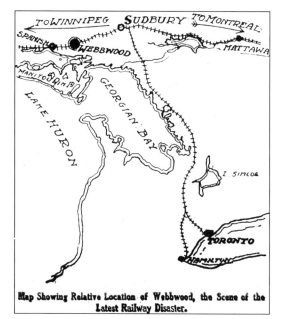

Map Showing Relative Location of Webbwood, the Scene of the Latest Railway Disaster.

river. The train had begun to cross the bridge and was travelling at about 45 miles per hour (75 km/hr) when things went terribly wrong. William Dundas, a mail clerk working in the express car, later described events:

> I felt the train pulling behind me in a very ragged manner, and I knew that the portion of the train behind me was off the track. For a distance the train pulled on; then I felt the air applied. I kept to the train when I felt her pulling up, and directly we were slowing down on the other side of the bridge, I jumped.

Probably half a minute passed from the moment that people realized something was wrong to the time that the locomotive halted. A great many things had happened in that interval. The rear wheels of the leading immigrant car had derailed first, and the following cars had whipped and jerked about. The first immigrant car, less half its wheels, had remained attached to the steaming locomotive and been dragged safely across the bridge, its occupants shaken but unhurt. The real horror was in the succeeding coaches.

The second immigrant coach had left the rails completely, slammed into a bridge girder, then broken in two. One half remained on the bridge and burst into flames; the other part plummeted to the river, smashed through the ice and vanished into the water. The first-class coach had also left tracks and bridge, falling directly into the river. The diner had rolled down the embankment, coming to rest with the front half in the water and the rear half on land. The Pullman car had rolled down the slope and come to rest on its side but clear of the river.

Eight workmen labouring on a nearby road bridge had witnessed the accident and rushed to help. Crewmen in the forward part of the train headed back towards the wreck area as well. Unfortunately the burning half of the colonist car on the bridge hampered access to the other side of the river.

Casualties were very heavy in the smashed colonist car and the first-class coach. One of the few survivors of the latter was P.J. Johnson, a cigar salesman. He vividly remembered the coach going into the river like a bullet, all the lights going out and water pouring in from all directions. The next thing he knew was that he was floating clear of the ice and shouting for help. He theorized that as the coach sank the air had compressed violently, blowing out a window and shooting him to the surface.

It was a day for heroes and heroines. Mrs. H.A. Linall of Winnipeg had sustained a head wound but staunched the flow of blood. Once she was assured that her son was safe she turned the Pullman into a crude first-aid station. She tore up clothing to fashion bandages and used whisky as antiseptic. Another passenger had been almost scalped in the crash; she treated his terrible injuries without flinching. Her performance drew praise from survivors.

Conductor Thomas Reynolds had been in the dining car when the accident occurred. It will be recalled that this car had ended up half in and half out of the river. Dazed passengers, covered by debris, were in danger of drowning. Reynolds braced himself and proceeded to kick out several plate glass windows which were still above the surface. He then led rescue efforts, shouting advice to some while freeing others from the maze of the wreckage. The car was settling, however, and the water closed over the exits he had created.

Reynolds struggled out a window. He found himself in a strange, terrible situation, with the ice above him, the car below him and the current threatening to drag him away. He wedged his feet in a window frame, tore out some fan lights in the roof and extracted two

40 KILLED IN C.P.R. WRECK BURNED AND TRAPPED IN WATER

Big List of Injured in Terrible Accident at Spanish River

HERO CONDUCTOR RESCUES EIGHT

Last Half of Fast Train from Montreal Fell Down Embankment—Diner and Pullman Submerged Under Icy Water of River—Twenty Passengers Reported Burned to Death in Second-class Coach

THE KNOWN CASUALTY LIST.

DEAD.

MRS. HOUDE, Sault Ste. Marie.
JOSEPH HEMAULT.
M. SPINKZEOMUM.
MICHAEL MIKENICLONKCO.
GEO. McILHENY.
FIREMAN REA&BRECK.
——ROBERTSON, C. P. R. travelling auditor.
FIREMAN LAVERY, reported drowned.
JOSEF MAROTT, address unknown.
Unidentified priest from Blind River.
REV. MR. CHILDERHOUSE, North Bay, superintendent of Presbyterian Missions.
M. LARADREAPHOPPI.

INJURED.

CONDUCTOR REYNOLDS, head and legs, not serious, North Bay.
THOMAS PARRISH, St. Paul, hands and head, slightly.
MRS. GEORGE P. DIER, Boissevain, Manitoba, internal injuries, serious.
MIKE NIKOLA, Max, North Dakota, slightly.
L. McDONALD, Minneapolis, scalded body.
E. MANSFIELD, Montreal, injured internally, serious.
D. M. BRODIE, police magistrate, Sudbury, ribs fractured.
SAM BULLARD, St. Paul, scalded

BYRON J. PEARCE.
Toronto Commercial Traveller Injured in the C. P. R. Wreck at Webbwood.

second-class coaches. Besides these the trains was made up of express, baggage and mail car.

SPLIT COACH IN TWO.

The train approached the bridge at a fairly rapid rate of speed, and the engine, mail, baggage and express cars were on the structure when suddenly some of the trucks jumped the track. The first effect was to split the second-class coach clean in two.

FOUR PLUNGED DOWN.

The engine, baggage, express, mail and one second-class car remained on the rails, while one second-class, one first-class, the diner and a sleeper left the rails, plunging down the embankment. The first-class car and diner went into the river. The sleeper and second-class remained on the ground, but the second-class car was burned. Engineer Trelford and the train crew, with the exception of Conductor Reynolds, escaped injury.

TRAPPED.

The descent was so sudden that the unfortunate passengers were caught

passengers. Somebody pushed an axe into his hands; he enlarged the new exit and dragged out more passengers. His efforts would later be recognized by the award of the Albert Medal.

B.J. Pearce of Toronto had boarded at Sudbury and had gone to a water cooler near the rear of the first-class coach just before the accident. As the coach began bumping along the ties, Pearce threw his arms around the water cooler. The fact that he was gripping an anchored object probably saved his life, for he was not thrown about as the car dived off the bridge. He was conscious of the impact, then found himself under water in a tangle of broken glass, smashed timbers and floating ice.

Pearce felt as through he was caught in a vise. He worked his way free of the ice, smashed out a ventilator and worked his way through the narrow frame. He reached the surface and tried to float on an ice floe only to have it capsize. He finally reached the diner and groped along it to the shore. Everyone else seemed intent on rescue work; Pearce set out for Nairn Centre for help. He stumbled along, pausing briefly to rest, then continuing. He had been joined by another passenger. They plodded on – the distance was too great to run.

Near the station they found a freight sitting on a siding. The engineer took them to Nairn, where they were lodged in a hotel, then he returned to the disaster site. When Pearce removed his clothes he found his underwear heavy with frozen, pulverized glass that had been ground through his coat and suit.

The crash had severed telegraph lines, so word of the accident was late in getting out. Although local help was at the scene about an hour after the accident, it was five hours before a qualified doctor arrived from Sudbury.

A summary inquest held on January 23 reported that the victims had died "from causes unknown." The Sudbury *Star* leaped on this, denouncing the process, accusing the CPR of "autocracy" and demanding a more thorough investigation. This prompting was unnecessary, as another, more formal, coroner's inquest was convened on the 25th and continued until February 4. In the meantime, the Canadian Railway Commission conducted its own investigation. These reviews were attended by some confusion arising out of the nature of the accident. The death toll was uncertain and much of the evidence was missing. Divers working in the icy river had to recover both bodies and wreckage.

CPR officials were annoyed at persistent press reports that 75 people had died in the accident. The figure was dropped to 63, then continued to shrink. The most commonly accepted final figure was 43 killed, including one man who died a week after the crash. Some 38 passengers had been injured seriously.

The cause and sequence of the wreck were also disputed. At various times it was claimed that the first colonist coach, second colonist coach and first-class coach had been the first to derail. The wheel trucks of the first-class coach were not recovered until February 4 – the day that the coroner's inquest concluded its work – and they were so battered and incomplete that little could be learned from them. The inquest jury suggested that the first-class coach had been the first to derail, but could not say what had caused the derailment itself.

The rails immediately east of the bridge were scarred with one rail clearly out of alignment. Clearly this was where the chain of events had begun, but had the rail been broken or twisted before the No. 7 arrived? Or had a coach suffered metal fatigue in a wheel and damaged the track as it came off the steel ribbon? It was a chicken-and-egg problem. Whether the rail or wheel had broken, it was another case of metal fatigue, and nothing in the disaster pointed to human error. No lessons could be learned from the tragedy.

QUEENSTON, Ontario

The Niagara Falls and Victoria Park Railway was one of the most colourful transportation companies in Canada. Operating from 1893 to 1932, its electric cars met Lake Ontario excursion steamers at Queenston, ascended the Niagara escarpment loaded with tourists, and then distributed them at the Brock Monument, assorted picnic areas and Niagara Falls. The view was superb everywhere, and for many years the company thrived. In 1923, its most successful year, the firm's cars carried almost two million passengers. The company's undoing was the expanding use of the automobile and extensive highway construction, which killed the steamer traffic.

Wednesday, July 7, 1915 was much like many other summer days. The war in Europe seemed remote, particularly to the hundreds of picnickers who had been enjoying the park. Among them were two large groups of Sunday school students and their attendants who had come from Toronto. The weather had been threatening, however, and about 7:15 p.m. it began to rain. The picnickers scurried for the electric railway cars, cramming aboard amid whoops of merriment. All seats were taken and standing room was jammed tight. A few even clung to the outside of the car. No railway official or mature passenger raised any objection to this packing.

The number of people crowded into the car, driven that day by Sidney Boyt (George Carswell, conductor) later became a matter of conjecture. The open, cross-seated coaches normally carried 60 to 80 people. At a subsequent investigation, when a company official was asked what constituted a limit, he replied, "All that could be got

WM. 2056 QUEENSTON AND BROCK MONUMENT 21 JUNE 1906

aboard." On this occasion the estimated figure was about 160! The overloaded car rumbled down the track, now slick with rain, and began to descend the 200-foot (70-metre) escarpment).

So steep was the grade that a safety switch had been installed near the top. Should a trolley car lose its brakes and career around the first curve, it would be routed onto a short siding and be stopped by buffers. There was only one such switch, though, and many more curves.

The lower terminus of the Niagara Falls and Victoria Park Railway at Queenston. In the background, at the top of the hill, can be seen the Brock Monument. (National Archives of Canada PA16661

All the subsequent evidence indicated that a series of equipment failures occurred within seconds. As the car was descending the route – and having passed the safety switch – the trolley's pickup slipped off the overhead wire. That robbed Boyt of the ability to reverse. Then the air brakes failed. Suddenly the car had turned into a frightening, rushing brute, beyond the motorman's control. The Toronto *Globe* account is as accurate a description as one can find of the next few seconds:

> The car immediately began to gain a terrible momentum. The screams and cries of the terrified passengers attracted the stupefied attention of those above and below. There was no possibility to give aid.
>
> Two of the sharp curves the madly speeding car negotiated in safety, though, and as it swept round them the spectators held their breath. On the third and last curve the car plunged from the rails. It completely jumped the tracks, and, wiping away a trolley pole as though it were tinder, plunged over the embankment. It landed upon its side, and ploughed for some few feet along the ground, striking a tree which split the car as by a knife.
>
> Contact with the tree completely wrecked the rear part of the car, and the fore part slewed for some further distance, leaving in its wake a trail of debris and crushed bodies.

Mrs. E.J. Smith, who survived, summed up the event most succinctly: "There was a crash and the car went to pieces like a smashed box." Harold Partridge, organist at a Toronto church, had shouted, "Hold your seats – it's off the rails," before his life was snuffed out.

The first rescuers on the scene were soldiers of the 19th Militia Regiment who had been guarding the Queenston-Lewiston International Bridge (Canadian authorities were edgy about possible wartime sabotage). More help, including military doctors, soon came up from the training base at Camp Niagara (Niagara-on-the-Lake). It required only 90 minutes to sort out the casualties. Eight people had been killed on the spot and about 95 had been hurt. Several injured passengers were despatched to Niagara Falls. Meanwhile, arrangements were made to convey the majority of victims back to Toronto.

The steamer *Chippawa* had been waiting at the Queenston Dock to receive excursionists. It was transformed into a hospital ship and set off down the Niagara River, crossing Lake Ontario to arrive about 11:00 p.m. at Toronto harbour and scenes of pandemonium. Three people had died aboard during the passage. Within hours, two others succumbed – one in a Toronto hospital, the other in Niagara Falls.

This diagram from the *Telegram* can be related to the preceding photo.

Two further victims, suffering multiple fractures and internal injuries, died on the 9th and 11th, raising the final toll to 15.

Richard Watson, age 30, had been killed instantly. An engraved watch revealed that 17 years before he had rescued a girl from drowning in Scotland. His luck had run out at Queenston. Watson had been travelling with his five children. One had been on his lap when the car left the rails; none had been injured.

SCENE OF THE TRAGEDY

WHERE CAR UPSET

WHERE CAR STARTED

Thirteen members of a family named Keates were aboard the car. Ten emerged unscathed, two were hurt, and one, a seven-year-old girl, was killed.

On July 8 an outraged Toronto Board of Control passed a resolution calling for criminal prosecutions. The civic politicians had not even waited for the convening of a coroner's inquest before demanding punishment. An inquest finally opened at Niagara-on-the-Lake on July 28. Among the facts brought forth was that the doomed electric railway car would normally have been equipped with a "sand punch" – an emergency device to sprinkle sand on the rails and assist braking. However, it had been removed for repairs prior to the accident. Once the air brake failed, motorman Boyt had had only an emergency hand-brake to stop the careening, overloaded car.

In the end, the coroner's jury was reluctant to indict either Boyt (an 11-year veteran of the company with an accident-free record) or his conductor, George Carswell (also with 11 years of service). They concluded that the "motorman did all in his power that was possible for him to do with the equipment at hand." Yet the jurors took a slap at both management and employees by noting a "very slack observance of rules of the company by the officers and operators regarding equipment, which includes sand and loading."

On August 15, 1915, a charge of criminal negligence was laid against E.R. Dickson, vice-president and general manager of the International Car Company, which controlled the Niagara Falls and Victoria Park Railway. At the heart of the case were the absence of safety switches on three of the four major curves, the operability of emergency equipment such as the sand punch, and the practice of overloading cars.

A preliminary hearing opened in St. Catharines on September 1 before Magistrate J.H. Campbell. The following day, Campbell dismissed the charges against Dickson. Some of his reasoning was sensible enough. He pointed out that the road was in good repair, the employees capable and the railway virtually accident-free for 21 years. A responsible regulatory body, the Ontario Railway Board, had never ordered any improvements to the line, nor had such action ever been considered by Dickson's superiors, the owners or directors of the firm. On the other hand, Magistrate Campbell expressed a disinclination to hold the general manager responsible for employee negligence or disobedience of loading orders, even when such negligence was a common practice. The reader may ask, then, just what responsibilities *did* lie with the general manager? One cannot help but recall the Komoka railway fire, when management was ignorant of employees disregarding fundamental safety rules.

The aftermath of the Queenston tragedy seemed to indicate once more that, where blame was to be widely apportioned, courts were loath to single out any particular scapegoat but were equally reluctant to confront all negligent parties. In the chain of command and regulation, from local supervisors to the Ontario Railway Board itself, many people had either failed to see or declined to report a series of factors which pointed towards a possible accident.

BRANDON, Manitoba

JANUARY 12, 1916

Manitobans take grim pride in their winter climate, alternately boasting about it and planning how to escape it. On Sunday, January 9, 1916, the worst storm of the season battered Manitoba. It was a killer blizzard, claiming a few lives and inflicting severe frostbite on many more people. Snow blocked the roads and trains were slowed. In the complex Brandon rail yards, traffic came near to a complete halt. Even when the storm abated, the numbing cold persisted.

Brandon was then a small city of some 10,000 souls. It was the commercial and industrial centre for western Manitoba. The community had been born in 1881 with the building of the Canadian Pacific Railway. The company had arbitrarily picked the townsite with an eye to real estate profits. The main street, Rosser Avenue, bore the name of the CPR's first chief engineer. Pre-war waves of Central European immigrants had touched the city, for although the surrounding farmland had been taken up in the 1880s by Ontario settlers, Brandon itself had attracted many of the more recent arrivals. The city was visibly divided between Anglo-Celtic "haves" and Slavic "have-nots."

In the days following the Sunday blizzard, the CPR was intent on digging out the Brandon rail yards. Winds and drifting snow undid in an afternoon what men had accomplished in a morning, but by mid-week the workmen were getting on top of the situation. On Wednesday, January 12, a "snow train" was at work – a yard engine, ten flatcars, a caboose, and roughly 50 men shovelling snow onto the cars for movement elsewhere. The foreman, George McGhie, was part of Brandon's "respectable" working class. Most of the men under him were stolid Europeans who spoke with thick accents when they attempted English. Few tried the new language; they swore, joked and complained in Polish, Ukrainian and other tongues.

With one portion of the tracks cleared, the snow train set off to another section of the yards. It was difficult to move around the labyrinth of tracks, some with boxcars or other rolling stock in place. E.H. Westbury, the engineer, had to take his train onto the main line before switching to another siding. The work train did not have an automatic right to be on the through tracks; Company Rule No. 93 stated that yard engines should avoid the main line when scheduled express trains were due to use it. On other occasions, however, yard engines had free use of all tracks in the yard complex. Since no express was due at this hour, 10:00 a.m., Westbury did not hesitate to venture onto the through tracks. To reach the next area slated for snow clearance he began backing in a westerly direction, pushing rather than pulling his train.

Some 30 of the workmen had crowded into the caboose, sheltering from the stinging cold. Among them was the conductor, Edward George Beal. He was concerned about visibility. The freight yards lay down in the flat, wide Assiniboine River valley, and a thick fog had blanketed the place. One could scarcely see more than two or three car lengths ahead. As a precaution, Beal ordered a brakeman, J.R. Henderson, to climb into the cupola of the caboose where he would have a better view of traffic. Yet even if Henderson spotted a hazard, he would have no means of warning the engineer at the other end of the work train.

Elsewhere in the yards, a livestock train was preparing to depart for Winnipeg. Initially it had been due to leave about 4:00 a.m., but another freight, stalled on a spur line, had blocked the way. More delays had been imposed by passenger trains running through. With the stalled freight still blocking access to the eastern switch, the stock train backed up to a western switch and thus gained access to the main line. The man who directed this manoeuvre was yardmaster John C. Richardson. To the stock train engineer, James Fairbain, he passed a warning that a snow train was working in the yards; the freight crew should be on their guard. With these cautionary words fresh in his ears, Fairbain opened the throttle. His engine moved slowly eastward, groping forward through the fog, a long line of stock cars strung out behind. The speed was estimated at 3 to 6 miles per hour (5-10 km/hr).

The situation, then, was a freight yard smothered in heavy fog with the stock train moving slowly eastward and the snow train backing westward on the main line. The crew of the snow train had no idea that a freight might be coming. The crew of the freight had been told that a snow train was about, but they did not know where it might be; Fairbain would later say that he did not expect to blunder upon it so quickly.

The fog was thickened by locomotive steam. It happened, too, that a roundhouse stood near the line, and the atmosphere in its vicinity was doubly dense with steam and smoke. If general yard visibility was only 60 feet (18 metres), it was down to 20 feet (six metres) near the roundhouse. As ill luck would have it, the two trains met in that small white-out area.

Up in the caboose cupola, brakeman Henderson caught a glimpse of the oncoming freight and shouted a warning. Freight engineer Fairbain saw the cupola when his locomotive was almost upon the caboose, and he applied brakes. The two trains, each moving at a snail's pace (their combined speed was no more than 8 miles per hour or 12 km/hr) did not so much crash as bang together before halting. The stock train's fireman was not even knocked off his feet. At either end of the accident – the snow train's engine, the stock train's caboose – people reported the most gentle of collisions.

If the snow train had had a boxcar adjacent to the caboose, the Brandon yards accident might have been no more than a minor bump, scarcely worth a report to authorities. However, the flatcar coupled to the caboose buckled, with the rear wheels rising off the rails, presenting the floor of the car as a giant slicer. The stock train locomotive did not crush the caboose – it rammed it onto the buckled flatcar, which cut through wood and bodies in one cruel, savage thrust. It was over in a flash. Brakeman Henderson tumbled from his perch in the cupola, fell through the splintered caboose, which had been reduced to kindling, and landed beside the tracks almost un-scathed.

It was some minutes before yard personnel realized what had happened and converged on the site. Doctors were summoned; an-other caboose was run onto an adjacent track to serve as an aid sta-tion; the dead were laid out beside the rails while attention was con-centrated on the wounded, suffering as much from the cold as their injuries. There was little difficulty in extricating casualties from the wreckage.

Fourteen men died on the spot; three more succumbed within a day, and in the next few days the toll rose to 19. It was an appalling figure for what might have been a minor railway traffic accident.

When a coroner's inquest was convened, it was called upon to in-vestigate the death of foreman George McGhie, "the only British killed" as the Brandon *Sun* pointedly observed. The deaths of the other workmen were regarded as secondary to McGhie's. Newspaper reporters were uncertain about how to handle the deaths of immi-grants; the Winnipeg *Free Press* struck a sympathetic yet patronizing note:

As the majority of victims are Galicians or of other foreign na-tionality, it is the more difficult to find particulars concerning them, but it is known that among the dead are men of the very poorer class who gladly took advantage of a temporary job in or-der to stall the wolf from the door. Some of them have large fami-lies whose sufferings promise to be very acute unless something is done for them in the immediate future.

One such was Ignace Kircharski, who was reported as having left a widow and seven children; the youngest had been born only five

BRANDON STARTLED BY TERRIBLE DISASTER IN THE RAILWAY YARDS

THE DEAD AND INJURED

At five o'clock Wednesday afternoon seventeen were reported dead at the morgues of the undertakers. Nine were at Campbell & Campbell's, six at Macpherson & Bedford's and two at Brockie's. Eleven injured are in the hospital.

The cold and snow which has been a boon to many idle men was directly responsible for a terrible accident Wednesday in which sixteen men lost their lives, and from the effects of which many more may die. The C.P.R. put snow trains at work in their yards clearing away the snow and to provide decent working conditions.

About ten o'clock one of these trains finished the work in hand and started for another locality to clear the tracks. In order to facilitate arrival at the desired point, the train backed onto the main line. It was an infringement of rules, no doubt, but such an infringement of rules as is made in order to expedite the work. Of the workers, who numbered fifty, about thirty had crowded into the caboose of the snow train and were no doubt enjoying the few minutes' respite from the hard labor and intense cold. Unfortunately for all concerned, an east bound stock train ordered out, came down the main line, gathering momentum with each turn of the powerful drive wheels. Out of the fog loomed the caboose of the snow train, but as it couldn't have been more than twenty yards distant when seen, the human cargo of the caboose were either killed or terribly wounded instantly.

The engine of the stock train crashed into the caboose where the workers were resting, swept the car-body clear and most of the hardy fellows met instant death as a flat car behind the caboose jumped up and cut through it like a knife.

From the round house near by a hurry call was sent to doctors, hospital authorities and conveyances. Conveyances rushed the medical men to the scene of the accident and willing hands pulled the injured from under the wreckage of the car the roof ot which covered them like a blanket.

As soon as conveyances arrived the wounded were loaded into them and taken to the hospital, but in the interval frost bites added terribly to the suffering of both

★ ★ ★ ★ ★ ★ ★ ★ ★ ★ ★ ★ ★ ★ ★ ★

★   **EARLY LIST OF DEAD**   ★

★ Mikoski, Alec., 19th St. north. ★
★ Boloski, 61 7th St. north. ★
★ McGhie, George, 340 Rosser. ★
★ Somerton. ★
★ Robeck, Mike, 54 14th St. N. ★
★ Lamonski, Anton, 29 14th ★
★ street north. ★
★ Moroz, Harry. ★
★ Lysostey, John. ★
★ Kirhakiski, 53½ 12th St. N. ★
★ Bityski, Steve, First street. ★
★ Rutkowski, Tony, 52 14th ★
★ street north. ★
★ Balawiyder, 13 Assiniboine. ★
★ Dryla, Joe, 101 7th street. ★
★ Bolinski, Wasyl, 2109 McDonald Ave. ★
★ Shamick, Anthony, 57 9th St. ★
★ Shinik, Sowerstran, 930 ★
★ Stickney Ave. ★
★ One unidentified. ★

★   **LIST OF INJURED**   ★
★   **At the Hospital**   ★
★ Renewni, 52 14th street. ★
★ Botsok, Antony, 125 15th St. ★
★ Mathew, Mike, 227 7th St. ★
★ Butinski, John, 506 20th St. ★
★ Messik, Alec. 330 19th St. ★
★ Moroz, Bill, 53 13th St. ★
★ Bunk, Mike, 117 7th St. ★
★ Boloski, Paul, 1st St. ★
★ Tacarcki, John, 53 15th St. ★
★ Malmazock, Andrew, 18th St. ★
★   **At Home**   ★
★ Beal, E. G., Conductor, Avenue ★
★ Block; internal. ★
★ Henderson, J., Brakeman; ★
★ hands and legs. ★
★ ★ ★ ★ ★ ★ ★ ★ ★ ★ ★ ★ ★ ★ ★ ★

REPORT ON CONDITION VICTIMS IN HOSPITAL

A report on the condition of the patients under treatment at the Brandon General Hospital at ten o'clock Thursday follows:

Damian Remewni, 52 14th St. N., city. Injuries to both ankles and wrists. Condition good.

Anthony Dotsok, 125 15th St. N., city. Wound of scalp and chest, and bruises of face. Condition good.

Mike Matthew, 222 7th St. N., city. Compound fracture of left fibula—Condition good.

John Budinski, 506 20th St. N. city. Fracture of femur, fibla and fibula, (left); compound fracture of tibia and fibula (right); fracture of ulna and radius (left). Condition fair.

Alex Massick, 330 19th St. N., city. Severe flesh wounds and fracture of right leg. Suffering from shock. Condtion serious.

Bill Moroz, 53 15th St. N., city. Compound fracture of right leg, laceration of left leg, bone exposed, feet frozen, injury to jaw. Condition good.

Jos. Dreylay, 101 7th St. N., city. Died from injuries.

Mike Bunk, 117 7th St. N., city. Injuries to head and scalp, fracture of both legs, fracture of jaw, shock. Condition serious.

Wasyl Bolinski, 2109 Macdonald Ave. Died from injuries.

Alex. Mikoski, 19th St. city. Died from injuries.

Paul Boloski, First street, city. Compound fracture of both legs, feet frozen. Condition fair.

John Tarcarcki, 53 15th St. N., city. Both feet crushed and amputated. Condition serious.

Andrew Malnazock, 18th St., city. Fracture of pelvis, left hand badly lacerated and frozen. Condition serious.

An Unknown.—Died on admission.

Funerals of Some Wreck Victims

Two Burials this Afternoon, and Three Others on Saturday Afternoon

Burial of the C.P.R. wreck victims was begun Friday afternoon, two of the Ruthenian Catholics, Joe Dryla and Steve Batycki, being laid to rest in the Brandon cemetery. There was a large number of friends and sympa-

TEUT AT

Rumors of O Connecti Montene Did Itali Mount I

MITCHELL F

Regina, Sask., ty minutes con preme court jury in a verdict of Mitchell (2) utte

The charges ag found guilty w forging an accou been made by or ing cartage made Mitchell. (2) utte ing it was a for by means of rail be false to claim ernment.

GOOD COMPA ASSURED E

Winnipeg, Jan. group system of the latest and m yet tried, nearly ized battalions ha of assigning the men, to some par will be designate manner.

This policy ha some success by battalion, which mation of an Odd appeal has been lows' lodges in th every indication will be obtained make up the desi themselves are c scheme.

      Printer

The same batt ganized a printer another has bee railway employee have expressed t in their lot with

days before the crash. His 17-year-old son had been part of the work gang and had been injured.

Reporters may have been insensitive to the "Galicians" and their families (as had been the case with the Japanese workmen killed at New Westminster in 1910), but covering a tragedy involving immigrants posed difficulties. Language was only one aspect. Another was that, with the accident occurring right in the city rail yards, survivors scurried back to their families amid the shacks that formed a proletarian jungle in north Brandon; there they would not easily be traced by newspapermen. Civic relief efforts on behalf of the stricken families appear to have been minimal; the load probably fell upon the shoulders of the immigrants' own communities and church congregations.

The investigation that followed was neither perfunctory nor zealous. Members of the inquest jury were sympathetic to both train crews, operating in poor visibility with minimal or no information about each other's movements. Everyone was aware that had the flatcar next to the caboose not reared up, the low-speed collision would have been almost insignificant. After two hours' deliberation, the jury reported back. To the extent that blame was allocated, it was placed upon the CPR "in not safeguarding trains working in the yards." Reference had been made during testimony that the snow train should have been protected by flagmen, and this seems to have weighed heavily with the jurors. Nevertheless, they made no specific recommendations.

(Facing page) The Brandon *Weekly Sun* lists dead and injured from the rail yard disaster. (National Archives of Canada NL19361)

ONAWA, Maine

The reader may look askance at this chapter's title and wonder how a wreck in the United States could be included in a book on Canadian railway disasters. In fact, the tragedy in central Maine was as much Canadian as American; the company involved and most of the victims were Canadian. The line itself ran through American territory because that constituted the shortest route from southern New Brunswick to Montreal.

In a sense the drama began two days earlier as the CPR liner *Empress of France* battled winter storms to enter the Bay of Fundy. Once it had to turn away from port. It finally berthed in Saint John on December 19, a full day late, and disembarked hundreds of passengers bound for central and western Canada. Some were European immigrants; others were soldiers returning from Britain. Many were the wives and children of Great War servicemen.

Considerable confusion attended the unloading of the *Empress of France.* Families had to assemble at dockside, retrieve and sort their luggage, then board the CPR's westbound No. 39 express. No single train could handle all the arrivals, so as one train filled and departed, another began loading. These were referred to as sections of the No. 39. Eventually, by the morning of December 20, four such sections were running from Saint John to Montreal on the CPR's tracks through Maine.

Despatchers arranging meets had a complex job at any time, but the confusion attending Train No. 39 and its several sections was particularly acute. None was running on time, and their schedules became ever more muddled as the bad weather continued.

To understand what happened, we must place ourselves in the position of the crewmen running an eastbound 33-car CPR freight, and particularly in the shoes of its engineer, William G. Bagley. This train had left Megantic, Quebec, about 6:00 p.m. on the 19th and had taken 12 hours to cover 91 miles (145 kilometres). Roadwork and meets with other trains had caused the delays. The freight crew was anxious to reach Brownville Junction, their terminal point, where a new crew would take over. That station, however, was still 27 miles (47 kilometres) further east. The weary, impatient crewmen were meanwhile having to deal with a series of orders being issued from Brownville Junction by despatcher F.V. Shaw.

At Moosehead, a station with no telegraph, the freight waited while the first two sections of the No. 39, running 80 minutes and 128 minutes late, passed to the west. Behind them came a westbound freight whose crew passed an order to Bagley. This indicated that the No. 39's third section was running five hours late. With that information, Bagley steamed on to Morkill, a station serviced by telegraph, some 18 miles (29 kilometres) further east, arriving at 6:57 a.m. According to the information available to the freight crew, that third section was due to arrive at Morkill at 7:05 a.m.

However, from experience that morning with other trains, the freight crew anticipated that the third section would be running later still. In this he was right – but the section had lost only ten additional minutes. In any case, expecting a longer delay affecting No. 39, two freight crewmen would misread their next order.

At Morkill the telegrapher on duty handed Order No. 47 to engineer Bagley and a copy to an off-duty engineer named Chase who was riding in the caboose. Chase in turn passed the order to Isaac Manuel, the freight's conductor. The new order read: "Third No. 39, engine 783, late. Fourth No. 39, engine unknown, run eight hours late

Barnard to Megantic."

All previous orders received by the freight crew had mentioned only three sections. Order No. 47 was the first to refer to a fourth. Conductor Manuel glanced at the paper, apparently without comprehending its contents, and handed it to the station flagman. Engineer Bagley misread it completely. To brakeman

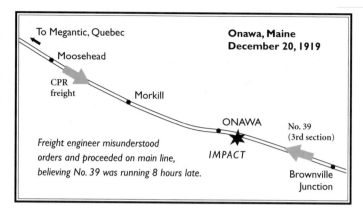

Earl Austin he said, "We have eight hours on third No. 39." Two minutes after reaching Morkill, the CPR freight was pulling out again. Bagley clearly believed he had a free track for at least another hour; he had confused the third section with the newly-introduced fourth section.

The Morkill station personnel, being unfamiliar with No. 39's complex schedule, did not try to halt the freight. At 7:01 a.m. they reported its departure by telegraph to despatcher Shaw at Brownville Junction. Shaw, juggling nine trains in his area, failed to appreciate what was happening. He thus lost his one chance to prevent an accident – signalling Onawa Station to halt the two trains. The express and the freight bore down on one another travelling at a combined speed of 100 miles per hour (160 km/hr).

Weather, a hill and a curve conspired to hide the trains from each other until they collided at 7:15 a.m., one mile (1.6 kilometres) east of Onawa. The Saint John *Daily Telegraph* later described the crash:

So great was the impact that the heads of both locomotives were crushed in until their bells were only about four feet apart. The cabs and baggage coaches were smashed to splinters. The first passenger carriage telescoped over the engine and the second coach ploughed through the tail of the leading car and mounted on top of the first. It was in these two cars that most of the passengers were killed or injured. About eight more passenger cars were badly damaged but they did not telescope.

Engineer Fred Wilson and fireman A.T. Henigar died in the cab of the express locomotive. Much the same tragedy happened at the head of the freight; brakeman Austin, riding in the cab, emerged bruised but alive, while engineer Bagley and his fireman, C.P. Hutchins, were killed. As was to be expected, the worst horrors occurred in the coaches.

Mrs. J. Bingham of Isabella, Manitoba, had been travelling with three daughters, ranging in age from two months to seven years. Ivy Bingham, the eldest girl, emerged with minor scratches, but the others of her family were killed. A Mrs. Petley, bound for Winnipeg

From the Toronto *Evening Telegram*, December 20, 1919.

THE EVENING TELEGRAM, TORONTO, SATURDAY, DECEMBER 20, 1919

15 KILLED AND 35 INJURED WHEN C.P.R. TRAINS COLLIDE

TRAINS IN HEAD-ON COLLISION
DEATH TOLL REACHES FIFTEEN

Thirty-five Others Are Injured — One Train Was Special Bringing Steerage Passengers from Empress of France — Bodies Now Await Identification

Onawa, Ma., Dec. 20.—Fifteen people were killed or burned to death, and many sustained burns and injuries to-day when a freight train collided with a special train from St. John, N.B., loaded with steerage passengers from the steamship Empress of France, on the Canadian Pacific Railway near here.

The freight train telescoped the engine and forward cars of the passenger train and the wreckage was burned. The engineers of both trains were among the killed.

The bodies of eleven persons were removed from the wreckage and laid in a row on the snow-covered embankment awaiting identification.

The passengers who were burned or injured are known to number 35. They were taken to a hospital at Brownville Junction by a special train which was sent with doctors and nurses from that place.

BOTH ENGINEERS KILLED.

Montreal, Dec. 20.—The C.P.R. issued the following official statement at 11.10 a.m. in regard to the Onawa accident:—

MUST HAVE CERTIFICATES

FOR REMUNERATION

Patriotic Fund Will Pay Allowance Cheques on Tuesday and Wednesday—Working To-morrow on it.

BUILDERS HONOR MAYOR

'LAUNCHING OF "T. L. CHURCH"'

Large Freighter to Bear Mayor's Name as Compliment to His Activities in Furthering Improvements.

SUSPEND WAR MEASURES

OLD ORDER RETURNS

Importation and Inter-provincial Traffic in Liquor and Horse-racing Likely After New Year's.

SHOT AT THE WRONG CAR

LORD FRENCH ESCAPED

IRELAND IS CALM

Police Searching For Those Who Attacked Lord French

R. C. CHURCH INTERVENED

CONFERENCE FAILED

Wreckage From Which Man Was Taken Fatally Hurt

The auto skidded when turning at College street and Montrose avenue at 12.30 this morning, and sideswiped the post. Wm. Goodfellow was fatally injured, and three women were injured, but the driver escaped unhurt.

MAGISTRATE REMOVED
FROM DONEGAL COURT

THERE SHOULD BE MONEY

FROM CANTEEN FUNDS

USE MIDDLE AGE TORTURES

TALES OF BOLSHEVISM

Refugees Tell Stories of Brutality Seen During Year's Residence in Soviet Russia.

Geneva, Dec. 19.—Nine Swiss citizens, of both sexes, including Mme. Jenni, sister of the Swiss consul at Kiev, have just returned from Kiev by way of Constantinople, and say they suffered terribly and witnessed the greatest horrors during a year's residence in Russia under Bolshevist rule. The Swiss party separated at Marseilles from a band of refugees, which included six British and two Americans and a number of French nationals.

TURKEYS EXPENSIVE, BUT—

Supply May Not Meet Demand For Christmas "Birds."

to meet her husband, survived with a broken leg, but two children, aged five and four, died. A girl named Phyllis Borthwick came through bruised but intact; her father and brother were killed. The final toll was 25 fatalities, including a woman who died of injuries on December 22.

Initial press reports were muddled. The Quebec *Chronicle-Herald* declared that the freight crew had let three sections of the No. 39 pass, lost count and then had pulled onto the line to collide with a fourth section. The truth was that the freight had struck the third section; the fourth section was hours behind.

A coroner's inquest quickly fixed responsibility on the freight crew for having misread their orders. William Bagley, the culpable engineer, had already paid for his mistake in the wreckage. An inquiry by the Maine Public Utilities Commission confirmed the findings of the coroner's jury and commented adversely on the Brownville Junction despatcher who had been overwhelmed by the confusion that morning. The CPR wreck at Onawa had been very much the result of human error compounded.

DROCOURT, Ontario

MARCH 20, 1929

Parry Sound, March 20. – Roaring through the night, two Canadian National transcontinental trains devoured distance. One steamed westward. The other was headed east. And they travelled on one track.

Suddenly – near the little crossroad depot of Drocourt, some 42 miles north of Parry Sound – the headlights of the two trains blazed terrifyingly into each other. The men at the throttles, with eyes glued upon the gleaming rails ahead, must have tensed – and trembled. The grinding of the brakes – the shock and shiver of the rocking trains as the "emergency" took hold, and gripped – the wild, shrill shriek of the whistles – the screaming clouds of escaping steam – the sparks of fire from the sliding and slipping of reversing wheels – the final, inevitable crash, heard for a mile or more, as the huge locomotives rushed together.

Another tragic disaster had been written in Canada's railway history.

Some one had blundered. Some one had failed. Some one had neglected or disobeyed orders. And the toll – the toll of death, of injury, of damage, of loss – was paid.

With these dramatic paragraphs, Toronto's *Globe* began its account of another Canadian rail disaster under a headline that screamed "WRECK DEATH TOLL AT LEAST 15, WITH 19 INJURED," followed by several layers of secondary headlines. The first of these read, "Speeding Fliers Crash Head-On, and Flames Trap Passengers in Wreckage of Colonist Car."

The Drocourt wreck followed a pattern that was becoming drearily familiar. The CNR's No. 3 Transcontinental ran daily from Toronto to Winnipeg; the No. 4 ran in the opposite direction. Under normal circumstances the two met at Waubamik, immediately north of Parry Sound. The No. 3, being the "inferior" train, would take the siding while the No. 4 continued through on the main line.

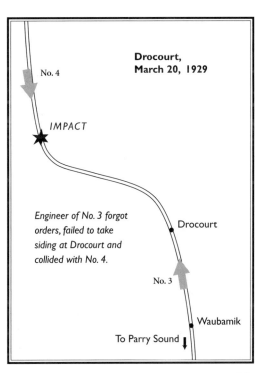

Drocourt,
March 20, 1929

No. 4

IMPACT

Engineer of No. 3 forgot
orders, failed to take
siding at Drocourt and
collided with No. 4.

Drocourt

No. 3

Waubamik

To Parry Sound

In the early hours of March 20 the No. 3 was running on time, but the No. 4 was some two hours late. Accordingly, despatchers arranged a meet at Drocourt, further north. The No. 3 would take the siding there to permit the No. 4 to pass by on the main line. Neither train was to proceed past Drocourt until they had stopped and recognized each other. These instructions were delivered to all running crew personnel on both trains.

It was a common procedure, but human fallibility turned it into a tragedy. At 3:57 a.m. the No. 3 rumbled through Drocourt. The engineer, G.V. Alexander, had forgotten his instructions. This was doubly puzzling in that his train was routinely the "inferior" train and thus regularly went to the siding for the No. 4. In normal circumstance the conductor, Ben Barstead, would have signalled for a stop, but on this occasion he failed to do so. Why Barstead did not act remains a mystery; he may have been careless, or he may have been preoccupied with other duties, including answering questions put to him by passengers in the colonist car. The fireman, Ernest Riley, suspected that the Drocourt siding had been passed, but as he had been on this run only two weeks he was not certain; he checked his timetable. In the rear of the train brakeman George Gorrie realized they had missed the station. He was reaching out to set the air brakes when he felt the No. 3 lurching.

About a mile north of Drocourt the track ran straight and level for some distance. Had the final approach been on that stretch, the engineers might have seen each other's headlights and hit the brakes. As it was, the track curved through a rock cut, and that meant that the crews would not see an oncoming train until the last moment.

They were about 1,100 feet (400 metres) apart when Alexander saw some light shimmering off the walls of the rock cut. He crossed his cab to get a better look. Suddenly he realized what was happen-

ing. He applied the brakes, then dived from the cab, followed by Riley. The crew of the No. 4, unaware of the danger almost to the moment of impact, stayed at their posts. Then, in a cataclysmic crash, two 6000-class locomotives flung themselves upon each other. There had been only 15 seconds between first sighting and the crash.

An express car loaded with fish formed part of the No. 4; it absorbed much of the momentum and saved the passengers aboard that train. The crew was less fortunate. Engineer Paul Gouvreau suffered two broken legs and serious scalds. His fireman, Horace Smith, was fatally injured. In the baggage car, express messenger Edwin Struck was also mortally hurt.

Toronto *Evening Telegram* coverage of the Drocourt crash, with an artist's imagined reconstruction of the moment of impact.

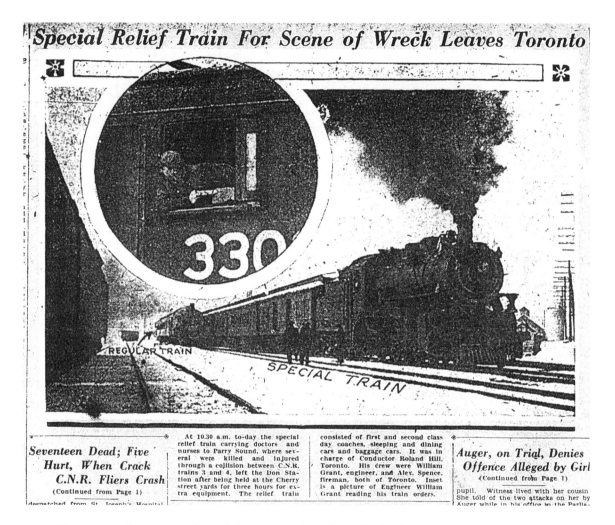

330

REGULAR TRAIN

SPECIAL TRAIN

Seventeen Dead; Five Hurt, When Crack C.N.R. Fliers Crash
(Continued from Page 1)

despatched from St. Joseph's Hospital

At 10.30 a.m. to-day the special relief train carrying doctors and nurses to Parry Sound, where several were killed and injured through a collision between C.N.R. trains 3 and 4, left the Don Station after being held at the Cherry street yards for three hours for extra equipment. The relief train consisted of first and second class day coaches, sleeping and dining cars and baggage cars. It was in charge of Conductor Roland Hill, Toronto. His crew were William Grant, engineer, and Alex. Spence, fireman, both of Toronto. Inset is a picture of Engineer William Grant reading his train orders.

Auger, on Trial, Denies Offence Alleged by Girl
(Continued from Page 1)

pupil. Witness lived with her cousin. She told of the two attacks on her by Auger while in his office in the Parlia-

The greatest havoc was aboard the No. 3 train, where the leading cars – a baggage car and a colonist coach – telescoped each other. The latter had a coal-fired stove, used by travellers to cook food, and it was the probable cause of the fire that swept through the wreckage. Survivors converged on the crumpled cars, trying to pull out injured passengers. Their efforts were not very successful; the devastation had been too thorough.

The No. 3's crew paid heavily; two brakemen were killed in the baggage car, while three others, including conductor Barstead, died in the smashed colonist car. The town of Galt would mourn the loss of Andrew and Winnifred Lockie and their two daughters, aged four and two; the family had been travelling to Saskatchewan to take up homesteading.

Precisely how many people died at Drocourt will never be known. Records of passengers, particularly European immigrants, were almost non-existent and the fire obliterated many remains. The lowest estimate was 15; the best guess was 17, and a month after the accident the figure of 20 dead was advanced as a possible (but unverified) tally.

A coroner's inquest, sitting at Parry Sound, ruled the surviving crewmen of the No. 3 to be at fault and recommended they be charged with manslaughter. They were arrested; bail for Alexander was set at $10,000, while for the others it was pegged at $5,000. A preliminary inquiry on April 15 confirmed the coroner's recommendation. On May 14 the trial began before Mr. Justice William Raney and a jury. Alexander was defended by Arthur Roebuck, one of Canada's leading criminal lawyers, a civil libertarian and future Ontario attorney-general and senator.

Roebuck conducted a brilliant attack upon a case prosecuted by half-hearted law officers. He quickly wrung from the first witness (W.T. Moodie, general superintendent of the CNR) several important admissions – that rules were vague in the sharing or division of crew responsibilities aboard a train (notably those of the engineer and conductor), that safe meets were more easily accomplished in stations that were manned (which had not been the case with Drocourt), and that a meet could have been arranged at Mowat, 8

(Facing page) When crashes happened in remote areas, help could only come by rail. Here the *Tely* shows the Drocourt relief train leaving the Don Station in Toronto.

miles (13 kilometres) further south, if delay of the No. 3 had been accepted.

Superintendent Moodie also admitted that an automatic block system could have prevented the accident; on this stretch of main line such a system had not yet been installed. The jury also heard Alexander's record – 17 years of service, almost all of it as an engineer, with two commendations for vigilance and prompt action in discovering defective rails.

Roebuck's greatest coup was his introduction of evidence that had not been presented at the coroner's inquest – statements by the accused engineer and fireman that they had been struggling with a balky locomotive that had distracted them from observing the approach to Drocourt. Riley explained that they had been crippled by a "foaming boiler," a condition resulting from sediment in the boiler which allowed water into the cylinders and threatened to damage them. He and Alexander had been forced to reduce speed, blow water out of the boiler, then replace it with water from the tender tank, all the while trying to maintain pressure. Being so distracted, they failed to notice Drocourt siding going by, and the dead conductor had not reminded them.

The explanation may have been a little forced – the problems described had not made the No. 3 run late. Nevertheless, Crown Attorney W.L. Haight may have damaged his case beyond repair by admitting that he would seek no penalties if Alexander was convicted. The trial, it seemed, was to fix responsibility but not to deliver judgement – in which case the jurors might well wonder why the proceedings were needed at all, given that the coroner's inquest had already reached its own conclusions.

Haight's comments and the judge's charge to the jury stressed that the engineer had responsibilities for the train's safety, that the conductor's apparent negligence should not excuse Alexander, and that the crew could have pulled their faltering engine onto a siding rather than try to fight their way forwards. Roebuck replied with all the eloquence he could muster, reviewed his case, and concluded by saying to the jurors, "You are asked to convict a man because he was not perfect." In his own way he thus admitted that his client had not performed his duties suitably, while asking if Alexander's negligence was tantamount to criminal behaviour.

The jury deliberated three hours through May 16, then returned a verdict of acquittal. The most remarkable aspect of the trial was that it scarcely resembled a criminal proceeding; it was a more thorough version of the coroner's investigation. Mr. Justice Raney himself criticised the despatcher's decision to arrange a meet at an unmanned station; the jury, having rendered its verdict, repeated the judge's criticism and urged that all meets be arranged at manned stations, at least until an automatic block system was installed on the line.

The trial wrote "finis" to the Drocourt story. Canada's next major rail disaster would be the outcome of nature run wild rather than human error.

CAPREOL, Ontario

JUNE 26-27, 1930

In late June of 1930, Mahatma Gandhi's boycott of British textiles was undermining Imperial rule in India. European and North American eyes were riveted on aeronautical events. Charles Kingsford-Smith and a three-man crew were completing an east-to-west flight across the Atlantic (with an unscheduled stop in Newfoundland) and were en route to a tumultuous New York welcome. Two Chicago pilots, John and Kenneth Hunt, were circling their home city, regularly refuelling in the air while piling up an endurance record that ultimately would tally 553 hours 41 minutes airborne. Pride of Arabia coffee was 49 cents a pound; Red Rose tea was 59 cents a pound. People tried to forget the deepening economic depression, but that was not easy. Already, thousands of unemployed men were "riding the rails," bumming rides on trains as they migrated across the continent in search of work.

Ontario papers were preoccupied with the terrible weather. On June 26 a drill boat, engaged in widening the navigation channel in the St. Lawrence River near Brockville, was struck by lightning. The vessel, loaded with dynamite, exploded, killing 30 men. The tragedy was front page news for days, relegating other disasters to minimal coverage.

In northern Ontario the weather was equally foul. Rain poured down – 4.25 inches (100 mm) in 14 hours. Fields were flooded, crops were drowned, and bridges, highways and railway embankments were swept away. Communities like Cobalt, New Liskeard and Haileybury were isolated. Trains rerouted to avoid one washout were liable to be halted or rerouted again as more track damage was discovered. It would be a week before normal communications were restored. In the meantime, this blind "act of God" was to trigger two serious railway accidents.

At 10:30 p.m. on June 26, the CNR's No. 4 express, running from Winnipeg to Toronto, was proceeding at some 30 miles per hour (50 km/hr) west of Capreol. The train had been on time when it left the previous divisional point, Foleyet, but since then it had lost 17 minutes, chiefly because of two "slow" orders issued for earlier points along the line. There was no such order for the section immediately ahead, a 700-foot (220-metre) embankment that carried the line over the swollen Vermilion River. All the same, engineer C.A. Virtue was running some five miles per hour (eight km/hr) slower than the authorized limit.

Other trains, passing at 6:00 p.m. and 8:00 p.m., had crossed safely over the embankment. The No. 4's engine, tender and express car negotiated the run, but everything went wrong after that. Following cars began derailing. Two – a first-class coach and a second-class sleeper – were hurled down the slope and into the river.

The two cars, lurching in a giant V-formation, each ended their tumble with one end protruding from the water and three-quarters of their lengths submerged. Pandemonium erupted; travellers who had been dozing in their seats or soundly sleeping in berths now fought the water that stormed over them. At least one man drowned in his bed. Three sleeping children were swept from their seats; their parents dragged them clear, but one died. Three other children were also drowned. Most passengers escaped through the coach doors that remained on the clay slope. Newspapers noted one heroine, a Mrs. Hayes of Hornepayne:

She was travelling to Parry Sound with her three small children. Without waiting for outside help or without losing her head for an instant, this brave mother broke through one of the windows and with a child under each arm and an infant gripped firmly in her teeth, swam strongly to shore, a distance of about 15 feet.

Engineer Virtue left on-the-spot rescue to others; he uncoupled from the second baggage car (which had tipped over) and steamed into Capreol to summon help. A relief train brought every available man. Most subsequent medical treatment was administered in the

THE EVENING TEl

VOL. LV. NO. 59   THIRTY-EIGHT PAGES   TORONTO, FRIDAY, JUNE 27, 1930

20 BODIES IN DEBRIS OF BL

Floods Wreck Two C.N.R. Trains, 11 Dead

Four Killed and 21 Hurt, As Two Cars of C.N.R. Train Go Into River at Capreol

THIRTY DIE IN RIVER BLAST

Tourist and Colonist Coaches Derailed as Result of Washout — Crew Rushes to Sudbury For Doctors and Nurses — Rescue Work Hampered By Flood Conditions and Darkness

Floods within an area of 20 miles in the district of Sudbury and Capreol took a death toll of eleven lives in three train wrecks on the Canadian National Railways last night, according to an official statement issued at noon to-day.

PRINCE, THE HERO, DIES WITH MASTER

Brockville, Ont., June 27.—(Staff Special)—To the list of those lives snuffed out on the dynamite drill boat here yesterday must be added the name of a canine hero, "Prince." No one knows whether "Prince" made any serious effort in the present catastrophe, but already he had a trophy for saving a life. And the man, John Wylie, whom "Prince" saved from the waters of the St. Lawrence some months ago, is also among the missing members of John B. King's crew.

town; another relief train from Toronto derailed in a washout south of Sudbury.

The wreck at Vermilion River killed five persons and injured 36 (21 seriously). Among the uninjured passengers was Doctor Thomas Stoddard, who subsequently acted as the investigating coroner. His inquest results, published on July 3, blamed a waterlogged roadbed where one rail had sagged, causing the lurch that derailed most of the rolling stock.

Headlines in the *Evening Telegram* announce the blast on a boat at Brockville that killed 30 people, as well as the railway accidents near Capreol.

The Vermilion River accident was followed closely by another. At 4:15 a.m. on June 27, CNR freight No. 401, westbound from North Bay, encountered a "sink hole" – a soggy, waterlogged patch of embankment – near Crerar, 26 miles (41 kilometres) east of Capreol. As the train started across the site, which had the consistency of a mud pie, the earth and gravel gave way and the freight lurched over in a horrific crash.

Fireman Albert E. McLeod was killed. Far back in the boxcars were about 18 non-paying passengers – "trespassers" in legal parlance, "hoboes" to others, "migrant workers" to more sympathetic folk. Eight were killed in the smashed wooden cars; only four would be identified by name in subsequent reports. Survivors scrambled out, rescued comrades, then moved forward to the locomotive.

They found a terrible scene. Engineer John M. McDonald, badly scalded and mad with pain, had been trapped with one foot jammed in the wreckage. He was attempting to free himself by desperate means – he was using a large knife in an effort to amputate his own foot. Fearing he would bled to death, the vagrants disarmed the engineer, then pried at the debris for 15 minutes before liberating him from the wreck. Their efforts were in vain; McDonald died of his injuries.

While the migrant workers were struggling to free McDonald, 36-year-old Clifford Boivin was working to prevent further tragedy. The brakeman had been wounded at Passchendaele with the 21st Battalion some 13 years before. Now, in spite of old pains and fresh injuries, he walked two miles back to Spindal siding to flag down a following CPR express. If it had continued on it would have blundered into the gaping 50-foot (15-metre) hole that had swallowed the freight.

It was a harsh time. The vagrants who survived the crash refused to give their names. When they asked for a ride on a relief train heading into Capreol, railway crews at first refused, telling the men to walk the rest of the way. Finally, compassion prevailed and the hoboes were given a lift.

The Crerar wreck was treated as a twin of the one at Vermilion River; Doctor Stoddard presided as coroner over both investigations. No blame was affixed to anyone; the freakish weather was deemed to be sufficient explanation. It reflected the times that the Crerar accident, which had chiefly killed transients, received far less attention than the one at Vermilion River, even though more people had been killed aboard the freight than on the express. Nor was this the last time that men "riding the rails" would figure as victims in a wreck. On July 31, 1937, the mid-section of a freight derailed 97 miles (140 kilometres) northwest of Sudbury. Some 35 transients were aboard; seven were killed and seven more injured by timbers rolling on top of them. By then the Depression had been recognized for the social tragedy it was, and media coverage was more complete and sympathetic to the dead and injured.

DUNDAS, Ontario

DECEMBER 25, 1934

The great wreck at Dundas, Ontario, on Christmas night 1934 resembled to some degree the Toronto High Park crash of January 2, 1884. Both were caused by human error and in each instance the person responsible immediately admitted his culpability. In the case of the Dundas wreck the human factor even managed to negate the presence of a fully automatic block signal system.

The story began with an eastbound CNR holiday special consisting of seven or eight coaches (accounts differ), which was running from London to Toronto. All of the coaches were of wooden construction, although the second-to-last coach had steel reinforcing. Aboard were 365 passengers.

Pulling out of the station at Dundas, engineer Norman Devine noticed that he had developed a red-hot crank pin. He halted his train on the main line and examined the situation with his conductor. Knowing that another train was following, they decided to pull the special over onto a siding where they would consider the problem more carefully. Devine sounded four short toots on his whistle – the signal for a brakeman to open the switch leading to the siding.

That duty would normally have been performed by Edward Lynch, the forward brakeman, but at that moment he was preoccupied in the coaches, talking to a passenger who had inquired about transportation out of Toronto. Lynch failed to notice the signal.

After a pause, Devine leaned out of his cab and shouted for a brakeman. He was heard by Charles Phelps, the rear brakeman, who was not at his regular post but was walking beside the fourth coach. Phelps did as he was asked. He went forward, opened the switch, and waited until the train had advanced onto the siding. He then closed and locked the switch again. Returning to the rear of the train he hung out red lanterns. The time was 9:10 p.m.

So long as the special had been standing on the main line the track signals would have indicated red (stop) to trains entering the Dundas area or block, and amber (caution) to trains entering adjacent blocks. The moment that Phelps locked the siding switch all main line signals reverted to green. These indicated that the main line was clear, which, of course, it was. The trouble was that brakeman Lynch, who should normally have performed the switching, was unaware that the train had moved onto the siding at all. His preoccupation with passengers plus the inky darkness had robbed him of his sense of location.

It is worth noting that the area concerned, some 200 yards (190 metres) east of the Dundas station, was not a simple one. Two main lines, separated by a hill, ran parallel to each other, and several spur lines branched off from each main route. In this situation, it was possible for Lynch to be confused and disoriented without being aware of his predicament.

After moving onto the siding Devine inched his locomotive forward slightly to centre the troublesome crank pin and make it accessible to servicing. Most of the crewmen assembled beside the engine, armed with grease, wrenches and water. After some discussion it was decided that the locomotive was unserviceable and would have to be replaced. Both Lynch and Phelps were present at this scene. Lynch volunteered to walk back to the Dundas station to telephone for a new engine. He began walking westward, towards the station and the switch.

As he reached the end of his own train Lynch saw a light far down the track. He knew what it was – the CNR No. 16 "Maple Leaf Flyer," the fast train from Detroit to Montreal. An idea flashed into his mind and remained fixed there: the special was on the main line and the No. 16 was rushing down upon it. He seized flagging equipment from the rear coach and began racing westwards, hell-bent to avert a rear-end crash. The No. 16 came on, seemingly faster than the authorized speed for the grade. It did not slacken its pace; if anything, it seemed to be accelerating.

As he reached the switch, 70 yards (65 metres) from the rear of his train, Lynch bent to work with unthinking fury. He unlocked it and threw it open. In his own mind he was certain that he had saved the special; the No. 16 would roll onto a siding. At the very worst a few boxcars would be smashed. What he had done, of course, was to switch the No. 16 onto the very siding on which the holiday special was standing !

Aboard the "Maple Leaf Flyer" engineer Bertram Burrell noted that all the signals were green. Strung out behind him were 15 cars and coaches; ahead of him was 65 feet (20 metres) of Northern locomotive, the largest in CNR stock. It was a routine run; the signals were green; nothing more than normal vigilance seemed needed.

He was applying brakes as he approached the Dundas station (no stop was scheduled), slackening his pace for a "slow board" just past the station where grade and curve conditions called for a limit of six miles per hour (10 km/hr). Burrell estimated that he was travelling at 15 miles per hour (22 km/hr) as he passed the station and that he was down to six miles per hour when he reached the board. Witnesses disagreed, setting the Flyer's speed at a minimum of 25 miles per hour (35 km/hr) through the station. At the board itself he released his brakes. The big Northern began accelerating on the downhill slope. Burrell's forward view was obscured by smoke and steam.

At the crucial switch, Burrell estimated he was going at 13 miles per hour (20 km/hr). Suddenly the engine lurched gently. Fireman John Kennedy, glimpsing what was coming up, shouted, "Soak her." At that instant Burrell saw the lights on the rear of the special coming up fast. He reached for the emergency brake, but that was more an instinctive gesture. It was 9:21 p.m. With no time or distance to spare, the "Maple Leaf Flyer" could not avoid impact. Instantly, Burrell and

Map from the *Evening Telegram*, December 26, 1934.

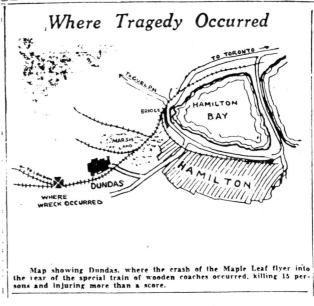

Where Tragedy Occurred

Map showing Dundas, where the crash of the Maple Leaf flyer into the rear of the special train of wooden coaches occurred, killing 15 persons and injuring more than a score.

THE EVENING TELEGRAM

L. LIX., NO. 208   THIRTY-FOUR PAGES   TORONTO, WEDNESDAY, DECEMBER 26, 1934   PRICE TWO CENTS

HOME EDITION

22 ARE KILLED IN TWO RAILWAY CRASHES

Wreckage of the special train photographed last night by The Telegram just after the Christmas tragedy at Dundas when the Maple Leaf flyer ran through an open switch, killing 15 persons and injuring more than a score.

Close-up of the wreckage of the two rear wooden coaches of the special, showing the terrific destruction. (Details on Pages 2, 11 and 12, with Pictures on Page 25)

Bullets From Bank Gun Unable to Halt Robbers Escaping With $1,500

Two Armed Bandits Put Staff and Customer into Back Room Dur-...

Best Choice for Mayor and Controllers

MAYOR

HUNT

BOARD OF CONTROL

Vote for These for Board of Education

DAY

State Misplaced Switch Cause of Dundas Tragedy

Ill-Fated Christmas 'Special' Forced to Stop by 'Hot Box,' Officials Report

Glasgow Prison Riot Causes 10 Injuries

NINE ARE HURT WHEN POLE HIT BY LOADED BUS

Cuts and Bruises Result of Skid on Lakeshore Road— Auto Behind Entangled in Wires

"Thousands" Send Greetings to Gloria

Two Crack C.N.R. Flyers In Smashes in 12 Hours; 22 Killed and 40 Hurt

International Limited, Delayed by Dundas Wreck, Kills Seven in Auto Near Chicago

Kennedy turned a hose on their own firebox to prevent a conflagration in the wreckage. That done, they joined in rescue work.

The CNR "Maple Leaf Flyer" had blundered into the rear of the holiday special – the very thing that Edward Lynch had believed he was preventing when he threw the switch. More than 140 tons of locomotive had crashed into fragile wooden coaches. The rear coach, shattered into kindling, was part-way atop the Northern locomotive. The second coach, the one with steel reinforcing, was partially de-

Railway accidents dominate the front page of the *Evening Telegram*, December 26, 1934. In a second accident a CNR train hit a car near Chicago, killing seven people.

molished. The third coach was heavily damaged, while the rear of the fourth one was smashed in. Passengers were flung forward and the lights went out. Then the screaming began.

As terrible as it was, it might have been worse. The impact uncoupled the last four coaches of the Flyer itself, and the air brakes held them in place. That probably lessened some of the brute momentum which carried the Flyer's locomotive 370 feet (110 metres) forward from the point of impact, ramming the special ahead almost the same distance (less the amount of telescoping). Brakeman Phelps and the conductor of the special, still working near their disabled locomotive, were nearly run down by it.

There was no fire – another mercy – though steam momentarily seared through the wrecked rear coach. Fortunately, too, several

Tely artist G.R. Snelgrove's dramatic depiction of the moment of impact.

WRECKAGE OF SPECIAL TRAIN IN WHICH 15 WERE KILLED

Telegram artist's drawing, showing how the Maple Leaf flyer crashed into the rear of the special train from London at Dundas last night, killing 15 persons and injuring more than a score.

doctors were aboard the two trains. They were able to give emergency treatment as the injured were extricated from the debris. Ambulances from Hamilton were soon on the scene.

Fifteen people were killed in the accident and more than 30 were hospitalized for injuries varying from bruises through steam burns, lacerations and shock to multiple fractures. All the dead and most of the seriously wounded had been in the two rear coaches.

The legal machinery set in motion by the crash worked swiftly towards a familiar end. On January 5, 1935, a coroner's jury sitting in Hamilton laid blame for the accident upon the confused brakeman, Edward Lynch. Upon the coroner's direction, the investigation was conducted narrowly. The jury was not allowed to comment on the implications of the continued use of wooden rolling stock for passenger transport. In this the inquest differed greatly from that which had dealt thoroughly with the High Park catastrophe.

Lynch was arrested, charged with manslaughter, then released on $10,000 bail. A preliminary hearing on January 16 committed him to trial, and a Grand Jury sitting on the 21st returned a "true bill" against him. From there the case went before a judge and jury for final disposition.

The trial itself was held on January 24 with Lynch and most of the other major actors taking the stand to reconstruct the events of December 25. The brakeman was ably defended by counsel. Much was made of the fact that Phelps had not been at his proper post, and that in manning the switch he had performed a job which normally would have been carried out by Lynch. If Lynch had been the man on the switch from the outset, he would have known the true position of his train relative to the main line.

It was Bertram Burrell, the engineer of the "Maple Leaf Flyer," who received the roughest treatment at the hands of the defence.

Could he not have seen the switch when he was 400 feet (1125 metres) from it? Could he not have seen Lynch throwing the switch? Was he not travelling faster than the rate authorized for the grade? Did not the fact that his train had travelled so far beyond the point of impact prove that he had been going too fast? At times it appeared that Burrell rather than Lynch was on trial. The engineer stoutly asserted that he had maintained proper speeds at all times, but the staff on duty at the Dundas station contradicted him.

The jury retired at 5:10 p.m. and stayed out for three hours and 43 minutes. Filing back into the courtroom, they sat down – all but the foreman, who faced the defendant. "Not guilty," he declared.

ALBERT CANYON, British Columbia

MARCH 2, 1936

Railwaymen who worked in the Rocky Mountains faced dangers that were unique along Canadian lines. The peaks stored massive amounts of energy that could be unleashed as avalanches, rock slides, mud slides and sudden washouts. In some years there were no casualties; in other years men died in ones and twos. The most terrible disaster had been on April 4, 1910, when hundreds of tons of snow engulfed a work crew in Rogers Pass. The men had been clearing tracks of snow from a previous avalanche. That tragedy claimed 62 lives. Although not a "rail disaster" as defined by this book – there was no moving railway stock involved – it haunted the memories of all who toiled in the shadows of the great peaks.

In the spring of 1936 rising temperatures loosened the snow in British Columbia's southern mountains. In one section of track between Farron and Midway, 40 slides were reported, depositing up to

27 feet (eight metres) of snow on the tracks. The main CPR lines running through the mountains were repeatedly blocked; some trains were running two days late. It was a constant battle between the track crews and the unstable snow which cascaded down the slopes, some of which had been stripped clear of timber by slides in preceding years.

It was raining on March 1 as engineer Percy Shafer guided his freight train towards Albert Canyon, an area of spectacular scenery

A CPR wreck near Albert Canyon in 1904. The western mountains offered the most hazardous conditions for railway operations in Canada. (BC Archives E-00342)

where passenger trains often halted to allow travellers to admire the view. It was also a section where avalanches were a frequent plague.

The CPR main line emerged from the Connaught Tunnel to descend the western slopes of the Selkirks in a 41-mile (62-kilometre) run down the Illecillewaet River as far as Revelstoke, where the Illecillewaet joins the Columbia. In that stretch of track the road dropped 2,282 feet (700 metres). Just east of the Albert Canyon station, at a point known as Downie Siding, Shafer's freight ran into a snow slide some 15 feet (4 metres) deep. His engine was derailed.

A locomotive was summoned from Illecillewaet Station, some two miles east of the accident. First it hooked onto the freight cars which were still on the tracks and hauled them back to the station siding. Next it returned to the slide site to retrieve the tender, which blocked access to the derailed freight engine. A swarm of men – regular employees and pick-up labourers – were busily digging out the engine and clearing away the snow which blocked the tracks. They were cutting a canyon of their own through the drift; its icy walls rose vertically on either side.

Hauling out the tender was complicated. The accessible coupling and drawbar had broken as several hundred tons of momentum-driven freight cars had banged forward in the original accident. A chain was produced, lashed to the tender, then looped over the salvage engine's coupling. By now it was 3:00 a.m. on March 2.

A.O. Alman, the freight's fireman, had been several hours at the derailment site and was hungry. He hopped aboard the salvage engine for the short ride to Illecillewaet, leaving Shafer behind, sheltering in his locomotive cab with several other men. As the salvage train moved slowly eastward, ascending the slope, three men were riding on the towed tender – Ernest Jones (brakeman), Andrew Sheppherd (car repairmen) and Bruce C. Calder (conductor of the salvage train).

A rumbling noise growled through the inky dark canyon, as though another avalanche was pouring down onto the tracks. The salvage locomotive's engineer hit the brakes. The towed tender came forward, bumping the towing engine. In that instant the chain securing the tender slipped its loop and came loose. The tender started rolling backwards, gathering speed as it plunged towards the cut in the drift where workers were still digging snow.

The three men aboard the tender discovered it had no hand brake. Jones and Calder leaped and survived. Sheppherd jumped too late and was killed. The salvage engine blew a warning whistle, but nobody seemed to recognize the signal. In any case, most of the workmen in the cut were trapped by the 15-foot (5-metre) snow walls that hemmed them in. Some may have heard the runaway tender in its rumbling, whistling approach. It was going at 60 miles per hour (100 km/hr) as it crashed into the cut.

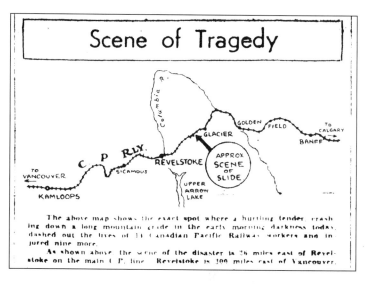

Map from the *Vancouver Sun*, March 2, 1936.

Two men in the locomotive cab died instantly; a third suffered fatal injuries. Engineer Shafer was pulled out by one L. Witall, identified in newspapers as a Finnish section foreman. In spite of a broken leg and other wounds, Witall performed heroically, dragging out fellow workers before scalding water inflicted further injuries on him. "His nerve and presence of mind," wrote one reporter, "is one of the outstanding features of the tragedy."

Sixteen men died in the Albert Canyon disaster, including 12 who had been shovelling snow in the cut when the runaway tender snuffed out their lives. The casualties affected a working community familiar with tragedy. The Vancouver *Sun* wrote:

> D.D. Cossar, divisional master mechanic, died of injuries received in the same place where his immediate predecessor, M.W. Boucher, was killed in a slide in 1930. Hans Haig, one of the dead trainmen, is survived by his widow, whose son by a former marriage, Orville W. Thompson, was killed near Downie in a head-on collision in 1929.

The nearest parallel to the Albert Canyon accident is that of the runaway flatcar in Vancouver (November 10, 1909). An inquest was convened in Revelstoke on March 4 and concluded the following day. The chain of events leading to the tender breaking loose was understood; the principal question was how securely it had been lashed to the auxiliary locomotive. Ultimately the jury affixed no blame to anyone, limiting its recommendations to a suggestion that safer devices be developed for improvised towing when regular couplings and towbars were disabled.

ALMONTE, Ontario

DECEMBER 27, 1942

The CPR's local Ottawa Valley train, the No. 550, was running late on the night of December 27, 1942. Holiday crowds accounted for some of the delays; not only were the coaches densely packed but more time than usual was taken up at each station as travellers boarded or disembarked. However, there were other factors. The night was stormy with mixed snow and rain. Moreover, the locomotive was proving troublesome with one tube leaking.

Crew members were unaware of any trains running behind them. They trusted that manual block signals would protect their rear from any unscheduled freights. In the meantime they struggled to keep reasonably close to their schedule. At 7:55 p.m. the No. 550 pulled out of Arnprior, chugged past Pakenham, an unmanned station this night, and finally reached Almonte. Normally the Arnprior-Almonte run took 28 minutes, and three minutes should have been spent in the station before pulling out again. Tonight, however, the No. 550 took 42 minutes to reach Almonte, and six minutes were consumed in the station. That meant that the express arrived at 8:35 p.m. and was not ready to depart again until 8:41 p.m.

It happened that there *was* a following train – a 13-coach special carrying Canadian soldiers. Orders had been issued to the trooper's crew to maintain a 20-minute spacing between their own train and the CPR local. Accordingly, when the special reached Arnprior at 7:59 p.m., despatching staff noted that the time spacing had shrunk to only four minutes. The crew waited patiently while fuel and water supplies were topped off. They started up but were signalled to stop, then to back up. Finally, clearance was given and the troop train moved off again. Departure time was 8:15 p.m. – exactly 20 minutes after the No. 550 had left. The trooper was to run at approximately the same rate as the local and thus take 28 minutes to reach Almonte. That, of course, assumed that the No. 550 was adhering to its schedule, which was not the case.

The crew of the troop train were a mixed lot. At the throttle was Lorne P. Richardson. Although he had worked some 32 years with the CPR, he had only recently been retrained as an engineer. Most of his experience had been with freights, and this was his first trip as engineer of a passenger train. His fireman, S.C. Thompson, was also relatively new at his job. The conductor, 62-year-old John C. Howard, was a very experienced man who had joined the CPR as a porter in 1906 and had been a conductor since 1911.

Engineer Richardson had his work cut out for him. He was responsible for an important lot of soldiers, he had to watch for signals, and he had to time his run to Almonte without a speed gauge in the cab. He believed he was running close to his scheduled time; in fact, he gained two minutes on the run to Almonte.

The reader may calculate exactly what happened that night. Starting from a 20-minute gap between the two trains, a series of events had eaten away the time spacing. The trooper ran two minutes fast – 18 minutes left; the local ran 14 minutes slow – four minutes left; the local spent six minutes rather than three in the station – the time spacing was virtually eliminated. Even with the trooper slowing on the approach to Almonte, a rear-end collision was almost inevitable.

There were two places where the accident could have been prevented. The first was at Pakenham, roughly halfway between Arnprior and Almonte. An operator there could have noted that the time spacing between the two trains had shrunk and halted the troop train for a few minutes to restore the spacing. However, the station was unmanned on Sundays, holidays and week nights. When the agent went off duty he simply set the signals at green. The engineer of the

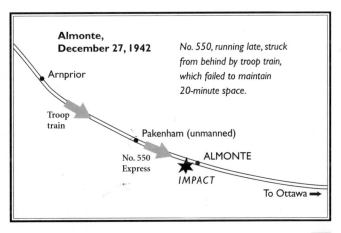

Almonte, December 27, 1942

No. 550, running late, struck from behind by troop train, which failed to maintain 20-minute space.

Arnprior

Troop train

Pakenham (unmanned)

No. 550 Express

ALMONTE

IMPACT

To Ottawa ➡

No. 550 and then of the trooper passed through with the blessing of a steady, reassuring green lamp.

The station at Almonte was confusing. A signal lamp mounted above the station was visible to approaching trains. One would expect that such a lamp would be red when a train was standing in the yards, but the local practice was that it would be green while a train entered the yards and left green until it pulled out; rear protection would be provided only by the tail lamps of the standing train – lamps that were frequently obscured by sleet and escaping steam used to heat the coaches.

The crew of the No. 550 might have put out flares and torpedoes (noisemakers) to protect the rear of the train, but outdated rules and current practice were that such action was taken only when trains were halted unexpectedly between stations. Technically, the No. 550 would have required such protection because the last two coaches were actually outside the yard limit. Certainly, if the local's crew had known of a following train they would have thought of such precautions. As it was, they were ignorant of the troop train further back. They reasoned that it was impractical to run back with flares when their own train was to be halted only briefly.

The Almonte wreck, then, would result from three factors – a troop train whose crew knew of the local but did not know it was running late, the No. 550's crew who knew they were behind schedule but had no knowledge of the following trooper, and a signals system that was ineffective at Pakenham and misleading at Almonte itself.

Thus it was that at 8:43 p.m., at the moment that the local was about to move out, the troop train rounded a curve and was confronted with the express barely 500 feet (133 metres) away. Engineer Richardson, who had slowed from 45 m.p.h. to 25 m.p.h. (75 km/hr

Still-steaming wreckage in the middle of Almonte. (City of Toronto Archives)

to 35 km/hr) on approaching the yards, misled by the green signal above the station, now hit the brakes and held on. There was nothing he could do. His heavy locomotive smashed through the two rearmost coaches, of mixed wood-and-metal construction, and crumpled the third coach before halting.

A few people standing on coach steps or the station platform saw the trooper bearing down and leaped aside. In the doomed cars the deadly force struck almost randomly. Here and there people were

killed; a seat away a friend might be injured; others were flung through windows and collapsing walls, sustaining wounds that ranged from minor cuts to major fractures and lacerations. So fully did the rear coaches absorb the shock that people in the fourth car from the rear felt little more than a jolt.

Fortunately there was no fire and no shortage of rescuers. Soldiers directed by Major H.C. Seagrim donned steel helmets and rushed to help. Train crewmen and Almonte citizens, recovering from the first

(Above) The town hall was used as a morgue. (Facing page) Another view of the scene of the disaster. (City of Toronto Archives)

trauma, began the grim business of tearing apart the wreckage for the dead and injured. The nearby town hall became a morgue; later it would be the site of the coroner's inquest.

Quiet heroism was abundant. Nursing Sister Anne Thorpe (Royal Canadian Army Medical Corps), working in the dark, treated some casualties and gave direction to persons wanting to help; her presence of mind would lead to her being decorated as an Associate of the Royal Red Cross. Nursing Sister H.M. Toner, another army nurse,

This dramatic close-in view shows the front of the locomotive (at the right) embedded in the wreckage of the passenger cars it hit from behind. (City of Toronto Archives)

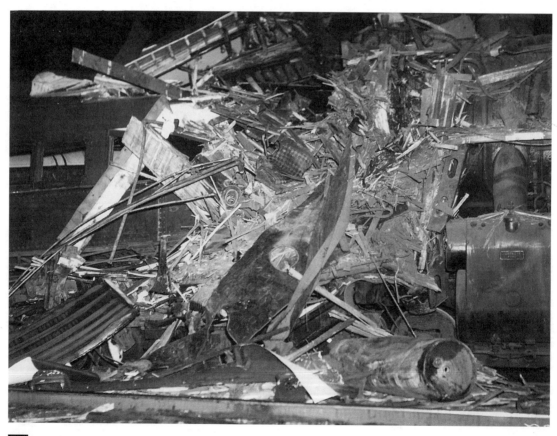

ripped the sleeves from her blouse to fashion a tourniquet, then tore up her underclothes to make more. Sergeant J.W. Gillespie, himself injured, administered first aid; his dedication would be rewarded in June 1943 with a British Empire Medal. Private F.R. Whitta would also receive a British Empire Medal; unaccustomed to surgery, he nevertheless helped doctors while stripped to the waist amid the blizzard. Three local doctors arrived, followed by more summoned from Carleton Place, Renfrew and other nearby points. Blankets for the dead and injured appeared from army kitbags and Almonte homes.

Two special trains were assembled – one with unhurt passengers, the other with casualties – and despatched to Ottawa. The latter train carried 84 stretcher cases and about 20 walking wounded. The *Ottawa Journal* described the terminal just as the mercy train pulled in:

> A scene reminiscent of the arrival of hospital trains at Victoria and Charing Cross Stations during the First Great War was enacted at Union Station early today when injured from last night's Almonte train wreck were brought to Ottawa's hospitals. For nearly two hours before the hospital train arrived at 5:30 E.D.T.* ambulances lined the snow-filled concourse adjacent to the station baggage room while stretchers and wheeled invalid chairs were lined up ready for the wounded.

It happened that Ottawa's Civic Hospital had been preparing for a year to handle some unspecified medical emergency such as an industrial accident. The staff were mobilized efficiently and subsequently won generous praise for their handling of the crisis. The fact that the disaster occurred during the holiday season helped; there were many beds left vacant at Christmas and these were filled by the wreck victims.

* Eastern Daylight Time; the continued use of daylight time in winter was a wartime measure intended to encourage industrial productivity.

The Almonte crash injured 155 persons and claimed 36 lives, making it the fifth-ranking railway disaster in Canadian history. It was surpassed only by the wrecks at Baptiste Creek, the Desjardins Canal, Beloeil Bridge and Spanish River. The crash indirectly claimed a 37th victim. John Howard, conductor of the troop train, wrote a note declaring he was blameless but expressing fears that he would be made a scapegoat, then drowned himself in the Rideau River two days before the opening of the coroner's inquest at which he was scheduled to be an important witness.

The investigation began on January 7, 1943. Doctor Smirle Lawson, Ontario's chief coroner, presided, assisted by Doctor A.A. Metcalfe, coroner for Lanark County, the jurisdiction in which the crash had taken place. The various lawyers present included Arthur Roebuck, KC, representing the Brotherhood of Locomotive Engineers. Roebuck, it will be recalled, had defended engineer Alexander after the Drocourt crash in 1929.

Conductor Howard need not have worried about being blamed. At the inquest the hardest questions were directed at representatives of the CPR who had failed to keep the Pakenham station manned, and the crew of the No. 550 who had not thought to guard the rear of their train with flares. As the inquest concluded, Doctor Lawson revealed his own thinking. He pointed out that the crew of the troop train had been given contradictory orders – to run a fast train, yet keep a safe distance behind the local express. Lawson described this as "liable to confuse any man" and further suggested that the green signals encountered would reassure rather than warn the crew. He concluded by declaring that knowledgeable managers should see that "necessary safety devices are erected to ensure the necessary safety of the public before a calamity occurs."

The inquest jury needed little persuasion or direction, but the members spent three hours drafting their conclusions. They absolved the crews of both trains of blame, ruling the CPR alone to be the culprit. They urged that the Pakenham station be permanently manned, that all trains slow to 25 miles per hour (35 km/hr) when passing through Almonte, and that an automatic signal be installed west of the Almonte station. As further emphasis on the latter point, they specifically recommended installation of a block-signal system to protect standing trains in the Almonte yards. The Board of Railway Commissioners, wise after the event, placed more blame on the crew of the No. 550 for having neglected to place flares in the rear of their train.

Occurring as it did near a metropolitan area, the Almonte diaster and the subsequent inquest were among the best reported railway events of this century. Consequently, the wreck is one of the best-known rail crashes in Canadian history, frequently mentioned and recalled when other wrecks happen. Residents of the Ottawa Valley are particularly conscious of their regional history, and the Almonte wreck is often mentioned as though it had taken place within the recent past.*

DUGALD, Manitoba

SEPTEMBER 1, 1947

On the night of September 1, 1947, eastern Manitoba railway despatchers had the routine task of arranging meets for the CNR's No. 2 and No. 4 eastbound Transcontinentals and an extra westbound train known as the "Minaki Special," which had been made up in northwestern Ontario. Summer was at an end; the resort areas around Lake of the Woods were emptying as families returned to Winnipeg. This

* Department of Tranport file 3202-7, "Accidents – Collisions and Derailments – Train Wreck at Almonte" found in the National Archives of Canada (Record Group 12, Volume 610) contains the report of the Board of Transport Commissioners.

Minaki Special, pulled by locomotive 6001, received several orders, two of which were particularly important. The first, No. 335, read:

> To Psgr Extra 6001 West at Malachi. Psgr Extra 6001 West meet No. 2 engine 6000 at Nourse and No. 4 engine 6046 at Vivian.

The special was clearly "inferior" to the regular Nos. 2 and 4 trains, and an "inferior" train (i.e., one yielding right of way) was routinely mentioned first in any order. When the No. 4 Transcontinental ran a little behind schedule, a more westerly meeting place was decided upon. Order No. 338 went out; it read:

> To Psgr Extra 6001 West at Elma. That part of Order No. 335 reading and No. 4 engine 4046 at Vivian is annulled. Psgr Extra 6001 West has right over No. 4 engine 6046 Elma at Dugald.

Engineer G.B. Lewis of the Minaki Special was an experienced railroader. He should therefore have understood that he had right of way on the single track from Elma to Dugald, but that at the latter point he would have to enter a siding and yield to the eastbound No. 4.

Shortly after 10:30 p.m. (Central Daylight Time) the Canadian National Railways eastbound No. 4 Transcontinental pulled into Dugald, a village some 14 miles (25 kilometres) east of Winnipeg. A few passengers disembarked and some express cargo was unloaded. The No. 4's rear coaches overlapped the western switch, where the siding met the main line; that line itself was occupied by the Transcontinental. Engineer J.R. Gibson waited patiently for the westbound special to arrive.

The Minaki Special, carrying 326 passengers, consisted of locomotive 6001 and its tender, two baggage cars, nine day coaches and two parlour cars. The leading baggage car was made of steel, as were both parlour cars that brought up the rear. All the other cars were of wooden construction. In fact, the CNR had bought no wooden coaches since 1923, but replacement of old rolling stock was a slow process. Wartime building priorities had dried up supplies of metal for new coaches over a six-year period.

The No. 4 was modern enough; the various cars and coaches strung out behind locomotive 6046 were all steel and all electrically lit. The same was not true of the Minaki Special. Some cars in that train were electrically illuminated, but at least half of the older coaches were lit with pintsch gas. The tanks for this gas, slung beneath the coach bodies, represented an explosive danger in the event of a wreck. The CNR was trying to replace this equipment; between 1930 and 1947 the number of gas-lit CNR coaches had fallen from 1,165 to 707, while oil-lit coaches had dropped from 601 to 308. Nevertheless, new equipment went directly to mainline work, and extra trains like the Minaki Special were made up from leftovers.

Dugald, September 1, 1947

Minaki Special failed to detour to siding and hit No. 4 Transcontinental, which was standing on main line.

No. 4 Transcontinental

IMPACT

Minaki Special

← To Winnipeg

To Minaki →

The special was itself running late, and engineer Lewis appeared to be trying to make up time. It was easy enough for passengers to compute their speed by timing the train from milepost to milepost. Those who did so agreed that they were moving at 72 to 75 miles per hour (120-130 km/hr).

There was a bend in the track east of Dugald, followed by a straight stretch of 1.5 miles (2.3 kilometres) into the station. Aboard the No. 4 engineer Gibson dimmed his headlight according to rules and went back to reading his orders. At the station itself, agent Donald F. Teddie gave the approaching train a green lamp, clearing it into the yard area.

That, at least, was Teddie's intention; it is not certain that engineer Lewis read the signal that way. His written orders were explicit – to take the siding at Dugald, clearing the main line for the No. 4. Yet his own conductor, Fred Skogsberg, had suggested to him that the No. 4 might be further delayed and that it was possible they would not meet the Transcontinental at Dugald. Seventy-five minutes earlier another westbound special had highballed right through the town when it was learned that a prior eastbound train had been delayed. The standard rule was, "When in doubt, follow written orders." Did that green signal confuse Lewis? Did he read the wrong message into it? Could he have interpreted it as permission to proceed on the main line, rather than mere right of entry to the yard area. Even so, how could he not have seen the No. 4's locomotive ahead of him with its headlamp glowing?

In the No. 4, fireman Hazen Lawrie was peering ahead when he realized that the approaching train was travelling much too fast and holding to the main line. He shouted a warning, then jumped clear, with Gibson close behind. The Minaki Special, slowed now to 45 m.p.h. (75 km/hr), suddenly applied brakes. It was too late. Locomotive 6001 buried itself in its twin, No. 6046. The time was 10:50 p.m.

The whole of the Transcontinental was hurled back 60 feet (18 metres), and the locomotive was totally destroyed. Fortunately there were no injuries there. The real horror was reserved for the Minaki Special. Its wooden coaches were caught between two masses – the engine, tender and metal baggage cars up front and the heavy metal parlour cars bringing up the rear. Three coaches rolled down the northern side of the embankment while a baggage car was hurled in

the opposite direction. In those terrible seconds the gas containers ruptured and flames tore through the wreckage.

Gerald Shields, a CNR employee living in Dugald, was standing 200 yards (190 metres) south of the tracks when the collision occurred. He was running towards the wreck when he heard two explosions and the leading coaches seemed to be swept by a blowtorch. He dragged out five persons, working heroically until his hands were cut and his arms blistered from the heat. He could not save a sixth per-

Dugald – the locomotives head to head, and because of their sturdy construction almost intact, while behind lies devastated rolling stock. (RCMP Photo)

son, a man trapped by debris who swayed silently in the inferno, dying in front of Shields.

Sergeant A.G. Clark and Private E.H. Tutt, both veterans of overseas service, had been passengers aboard the No. 4. Rushing forward, they discovered a scene more horrible than any they had witnessed in Europe. Together they dragged out two bodies and rescued two other persons before the intense heat forced them back.

One of the leading coaches of the Minaki Special included among its passengers Mr. and Mrs. Harry Irvine, Mrs. Larry Jarman, and Mr. and Mrs. William McAuley. They were sitting in one area with three girls across the aisle. Mr. Irvine later testified about his experience:

> We could feel the air brakes being jammed on. Bill spoke about them. Then we felt an impact. There was a slight bump as if the brakes were being slammed on again. Then there was a tremendous crack and the lights in the coach went out. Sparks were flying and there were some shouts. Our coach went on its side in the ditch. The girls landed on top of us. I knocked my head on a coat rack. There was a terrific noise of steam coming out of the boilers; it drowned out everything else.
>
> McAuley, who seemed cool, broke a window and got his wife out. I passed my wife and Mrs. Jarman out. McAuley went back into the coach and took out some coats.
>
> Our coach landed beside another which burst into flames. We moved into a field about 200 yards away. A couple of soldiers and other male passengers were evacuating women from the coaches.

As if the burning train were not enough, the scene was further complicated by flames spreading to a grain elevator and an oil shed. Virtually all rescue work was completed within five minutes, but the

additional fires, fuelled by exploding oil drums, hampered fire fighters, who arrived from Transcona. Most of the dead, trapped in the wreckage, were burned beyond recognition. They had to be identified through rings, watches and fingerprints.

Corporal C.M. Hartley, RCMP, rushed from Transcona and was on the scene ten minutes after the crash. He established a casualty station in the Dugald dance hall while summoning help from Winnipeg. Ambulances, police cars and other emergency vehicles converged on the village. Hundreds of curious people also headed for the

The frame of a passenger car smoulders in the aftermath of the Dugald collision. (RCMP Photo)

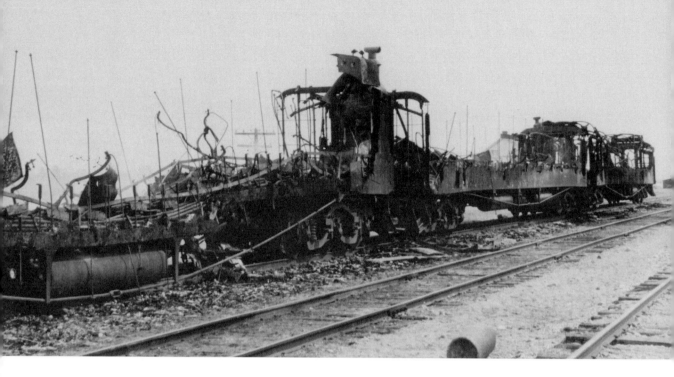

rail yards. Police were hard pressed to control the traffic, keeping all but rescue workers away from the scene and clearing highway routes for ambulances.

Another view of burned-out cars at Dugald. (RCMP Photo)

The initial estimate was 35 dead, but that was uncertain given the confusion. Over the next few days some of the "missing" turned up alive; a family which had intended to board the train at Minaki was found to have missed the special by minutes. The final toll was 31 persons, including four members of the Minaki Special's crew who might have been able to explain the disaster – G.B. Lewis (engineer), Fred Skogsberg (conductor), G. Rougeau (front end brakeman) and E.J. Papkie (fireman). Virtually all the dead came from Winnipeg and its environs. In two instances, four persons of the same family were killed; in three other cases, death claimed three members of the same family.

Attention at the subsequent inquests was rivetted upon Donald Teddie, the man who had given the green signal to the approaching Minaki Special. For his part, Teddie refused to play the part of scapegoat, and he was ably supported by his lawyer, Louis St. George Stubbs, a Manitoba legend who gloried in his reputation as champion of the underdog. He was up against another formidable legal figure – A.K. Dysart, assistant general counsel for the CNR and soon to be appointed a judge of the Manitoba Court of Appeals.

There was some speculation that the 63-year-old engineer of the Minaki Special might have suffered a heart attack just before the accident; similar circumstances were suggested immediately following the 1986 rail disaster at Hinton, Alberta. It seems unlikely that it happened that way, for Lewis had been removed alive from the wreck and had died an hour later en route to hospital.

On October 20, 1947, the Federal Board of Transport Commissioners announced its findings. Primary blame was placed upon the crew of the Minaki Special for having disobeyed written orders and running at excessive speed while approaching the Dugald yards. However, they noted that the CNR had placed wooden coaches between metal ones. The commissioners declared "an order will issue requiring all railways to marshall passenger equipment in such a manner that no wooden coaches carrying passengers will be placed between other cars of steel construction and that all wooden coaches will be placed on the rear of the train."

This measure was not always followed; the subsequent accident at Canoe River in November 1950 reminded officials that rolling stock could not be coupled randomly.

A coroner's jury had earlier recommended that flammable gases be discontinued in lighting railway coaches. The Board of Transport Commissioners concurred in this, and instructions to that effect followed directly.*

CANOE RIVER, British Columbia

NOVEMBER 21, 1950

Operation "Sawhorse" began on Sunday, November 19, 1950. "Sawhorse" was the movement of some 700 soldiers of the 2nd Regiment, Royal Canadian Horse Artillery, from Camp Shilo, Manitoba, to Fort Lewis, Washington, and thence to Korea. Two special trains were involved, running westward over the monotonous prairies, then through the Yellowhead Pass to penetrate the Rocky Mountains. The second train contained 23 officers and 315 other ranks, all under the charge of Major Francis P. Leask.

In mid-morning of November 21 the principal Kamloops despatcher, A.E. Tisdale, sat down to telephone instructions to points along the CNR main line. Tisdale had a fairly routine job to do – to arrange for the passage of the eastbound CNR Nos. 2 and 4 Trans–continentals past the second westbound troop train. Tisdale rang up the Red Pass and Blue River stations and began dictating his instructions: "Passenger extra 3538 west to meet No. 2 engine 6004 at Cedarside and No. 4 engine 6057 Gosnell."

Alfred J. Atherton, the 22-year-old operator at Red Pass, began taking down the message. For a few seconds Tisdale's voice faded, then came back clear. The operator read back the message; Tisdale acknowledged it. Frank Parsons at Blue River also repeated the order which Tisdale confirmed. Everything seemed to be correct – but in

* Department of Tranport file 3202-8, "Accidents – Collisions and Derailments – Dugald, Manitoba" found in the National Archives of Canada (Record Group 12, Volume 610) contains the report of the Board of Transport Commissioners on this accident.

fact, something had gone wrong. When the troop train pulled into Red Pass station, conductor John A. Mainprize received an order from Atherton. It read: "Passenger extra 3538 meet No. 2 engine 6004 and No. 4 engine 6057 Gosnell."

Missing from this message were two crucial words – "at Cedarside." This was particularly serious because the troop train was about to enter an 18-mile (30-kilometre) stretch that had no automatic block signal system – the only portion of CNR main line in the mountains not protected by this device.

How had Atherton come to hand an incomplete order to Mainprize? In subsequent investigations, the Red Pass operator claimed he had read back the order – less "at Cedarside" – to Tisdale and that Tisdale had not corrected him. If true, that would have made the Kamloops despatcher the negligent party. Tisdale, in his turn, declared that Atherton had read back the complete order. It would have been one man's word against the other, but the Blue River operator had been on the line at the same time. Parsons backed up Tisdale's version of events; Atherton would be cast firmly as the culprit in this affair.

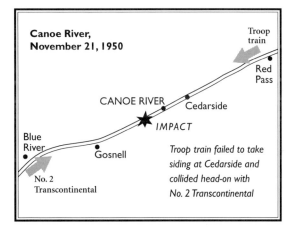

Canoe River,
November 21, 1950

Troop train

Red Pass

CANOE RIVER   Cedarside

★   IMPACT

Blue River

Gosnell

No. 2 Transcontinental

Troop train failed to take siding at Cedarside and collided head-on with No. 2 Transcontinental

The special train steamed out of Red Pass and began winding its way through the spectacular mountain scenery. It rattled along at some 25-30 miles per hour (40-50 km/hr), directly past the Cedarside switch where it should have taken the siding, and on past the Canoe River siding. Rounding a curve, engineer J.J. Stimson was startled to discover another locomotive, the No. 2 Transcontinental, not more than 550 feet (140 metres) away. Both engines began whistling while their engineers reached for the brakes. It was too late; perhaps only ten seconds elapsed between sighting and impact. The valley echoed with the metallic crash of engine against engine as two steel monsters demolished each other in a cataclysmic embrace. The time was 10:40 a.m.

Further south along the line, from the vantage point of an embankment, Thomas W. Tindall, a forestry employee, had seen both trains approaching, blind to each other's presence. He had waved frantically to the Transcontinental crew, who acknowledged his presence with a friendly return wave. Tindall was the last hope of preventing the tragedy to which he now became a witness.

The No. 2 Transcontinental consisted of ten cars and coaches, all of modern construction. The train was moving at about 30 miles per hour (50 km/hr) and descending a gentle grade when the collision occurred. All these factors contributed to preventing injuries; there was no slack between the coaches at the moment of impact, and the whole train absorbed the shock more or less evenly.

Aboard the trooper, however, the reverse situation held true. The 16 coaches, baggage cars and caboose – some all-metal, others of mixed steel and wood construction – were strung out on the uphill grade, with enough slack in the couplings to ensure that momentum turned the crash into a series of small, vicious collisions.

Gunner Malcolm McComb had been playing solitaire when the train began jerking. Everything went black. He crashed through a partition. When he regain consciousness he was in the coach immediately ahead of the one in which he had been riding.

McComb was lucky to survive; so were Gunners William Barton and Roger Bowe, both from Newfoundland. They had been buying cigarettes at the newsstand on the troop train when the crash came. They were bowled off their feet as the coach caved in around them.

The structure housing the newsstand saved them, supporting debris that would otherwise have pinned them to the floor. A short distance away Gunners James J. White and Joseph Thistle, also of Newfoundland, has been less fortunate; unprotected by anything comparable to the newsstand, they were buried in the wreckage.

In the forward part of the train the locomotive belched scalding water and a searing cloud of steam. The baggage car and three

The wreck on the banks of the Canoe River, snapped by an anonymous soldier. (Royal Canadian Artillery Museum, CFB Shilo, Manitoba)

coaches were flung off the rails and tumbled down a 45-foot (14-metre) embankment. Telephone and telegraph wires were torn away, but soldiers quickly spliced them together and flashed word of the wreck to nearby stations, using an emergency telephone set found aboard the Transcontinental.

Many aboard the two trains believed they had hit a landslide; conductor Mainprize initially thought they had struck the rear of the troop train that had preceded them along the route. From both trains people poured out to see what had happened. They stared at the point of impact, where the upended locomotives and tenders made a pile of junk 30 feet (9 metres) high.

There were no doctors aboard the special, a fact that was later to attract adverse comment. The Transcontinental had among its passengers Doctor P. J. Kimmett of Edson and a nurse, Mrs. J. T. Richardson of Vancouver. They took charge of the situation. Sleeping and dining cars were turned into first aid stations. The troops pitched in with cool efficiency, extracting comrades from smashed coaches, tearing sheets into dressings, helping in every way they could. Major Leask was impressed by Doctor Kimmett's work – "We couldn't have gotten along without him" – but he was equally generous in praising his men. Veterans and raw recruits alike behaved with exemplary discipline and initiative.

The wreck had happened in one of the most remote sections of the CNR system, 29 miles (48 kilometres) south of Mount Robson. Four hours elapsed before a relief train arrived from Jasper. Another train was despatched from Edmonton with four surgeons, five interns, six nurses and 12 medical assistants; they met the relief train at Edson. The most serious cases were hospitalized at Jasper and Edmonton; uninjured soldiers were taken to the Canadian army base at Wainwright, Alberta.

The engineers and firemen of the two locomotives were killed on the spot, as were 12 soldiers, four of whose bodies were never recovered. Four soldiers died aboard the relief train after leaving Canoe River, and one more died in hospital. The total, then, was 21 dead. Six train crewmen and 52 soldiers survived with various injuries. Burns caused by steam were particularly acute, and ten victims received special treatment at Edmonton's University Hospital. However, most fatalities involved soldiers with severe head wounds as well as scalds.

Subsequent investigations were complicated by an oil fire that broke out in the wreckage the morning after the crash. It gutted most coaches and probably accounted for the unrecovered bodies.

Atherton was identified as having caused the accident through his incomplete transcription of the meet order that should have put the troop train into the Cedarside siding. He was duly charged with manslaughter; his trial opened on May 9, 1951, in Prince George, British Columbia.

The trial was to prove one of the most unusual in Canadian history. Atherton was represented by three lawyers, but one dominated the proceedings – John George Diefenbaker, KC, MP. Although he was counted as being among the top criminal counsel in the country, he had not been a member of the British Columbia Bar until asked to defend the station agent. Diefenbaker had put down $1,500 and submitted himself to what turned out to be a perfunctory Bar examination.

The prosecution was conducted by the Deputy Attorney General of British Columbia, Colonel Eric Peppler. A veteran of the First World War, Peppler looked like the distinguished officer he had been, and people called him "Colonel" more easily than "Mister." Diefenbaker turned these characteristics to the advantage of the defence; a jury would have to convict Atherton, and Diefenbaker chose

to turn the court room into a theatre with his client cast as a perse-
cuted victim of "the big guys."

Atherton was charged with causing the death of only one man –
Henry Proskunik, the fireman of the troop train. Diefenbaker went
after Crown witnesses, many of them CNR employees, badgering
them about various subjects including the methods by which the
railway transmitted its orders. Colonel Peppler protested. "The CNR
is not on trial here," he stated. "It is the poor man in the box."
Diefenbaker retorted that perhaps the railway company should be in
the dock.

The coaches used in making up the troop train drew the lawyer's
particular interest. Some coaches had been made of wood on steel
underframes, others were wood with steel underframes and metal
sheeting, and these cars were sandwiched between all-steel cars.
Diefenbaker depicted the older-style cars as being decidedly inferior
vehicles, so bad that troops would consider any discomfort encountered in Korea as being no worse than travelling in CNR cars. Such
coaches had indeed been withdrawn from use on scheduled transcontinental trains; Atherton's defence lawyer suggested that the company had relegated them to what it regarded as inferior clients – Canadian soldiers. Diefenbaker's tactics set the courtroom throbbing as
Crown counsel remonstrated and spectators murmured to one another.

Strictly speaking, the CNR had broken no rules in making up the
troop train. General Order No. 707, promulgated by the Board of
Transport Commissioners following the Dugald wreck, stated that
passenger trains should be marshalled in such a manner that no
wooden coaches carrying passengers should be placed between steel
cars; wooden coaches carrying passengers would be coupled to the
rear of trains. However, General Order No. 707 specified that coaches

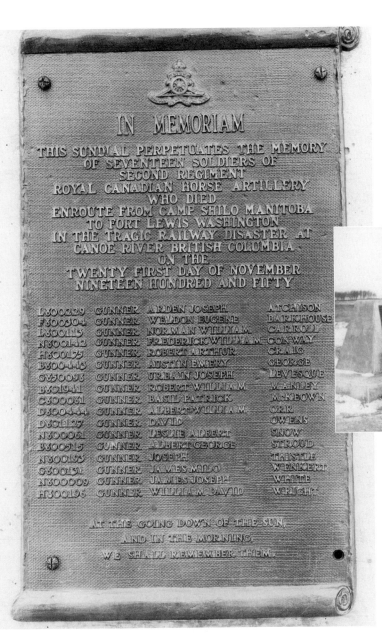

Two views of the Shilo memorial to victims of the Canoe River disaster. (Royal Canadian Artillery Museum, CFB Shilo, Manitoba)

IN MEMORIAM

THIS SUNDIAL PERPETUATES THE MEMORY
OF SEVENTEEN SOLDIERS OF
SECOND REGIMENT
ROYAL CANADIAN HORSE ARTILLERY
WHO DIED
ENROUTE FROM CAMP SHILO MANITOBA
TO FORT LEWIS WASHINGTON
IN THE TRAGIC RAILWAY DISASTER AT
CANOE RIVER BRITISH COLUMBIA
ON THE
TWENTY FIRST DAY OF NOVEMBER
NINETEEN HUNDRED AND FIFTY

L300229	GUNNER	ARDEN JOSEPH	ATCHISON
F80030-4	GUNNER	WELDON EUGENE	BARKHOUSE
L300113	GUNNER	NORMAN WILLIAM	CARROLL
N300142	GUNNER	FREDERICK WILLIAM M	CONWAY
H300175	GUNNER	ROBERT ARTHUR	CRAIG
B300445	GUNNER	AUSTIN EMERY	GEORGE
G450093	GUNNER	URBAIN JOSEPH	LEVESQUE
B301941	GUNNER	ROBERT WILLIAM	MANLEY
C300081	GUNNER	BASIL PATRICK	McKEOWN
D300444	GUNNER	ALBERT WILLIAM	ORR
D30127	GUNNER	DAVID	OWENS
N300061	GUNNER	LESLIE ALBERT	SNOW
B300515	GUNNER	ALBERT GEORGE	STROUD
N300195	GUNNER	JOSEPH	THISTLE
C300131	GUNNER	JAMES MILO	WEINKERT
N300009	GUNNER	JAMES JOSEPH	WHITE
H300196	GUNNER	WILLIAM DAVID	WRIGHT

AT THE GOING DOWN OF THE SUN,
AND IN THE MORNING,
WE SHALL REMEMBER THEM.

with steel underframes should *not* be classified as wooden coaches, at least for the aims of that particular rule.

The coaches, of course, had nothing to do with the death of the fireman – the victim named in the indictment – and the prosecutor tried to drag the court back to that point.

"We want to make it clear," he remarked, "that in this case we are not concerned about the death of a few privates going to Korea." That careless sentence provoked Diefenbaker's finest court-room wrath.

"You're not concerned about the killing of a few privates! Oh Colonel!"

One juror, a veteran of the First World War, was heard saying to another, "Did you hear what that bastard said?"

The trial was only halfway done, but Diefenbaker had already won; his subsequent tactics simply guaranteed victory. He repeatedly called the prosecutor "Colonel." He hinted darkly of a CNR plot to make Atherton a scapegoat; a pre-trial meeting of CNR witnesses he described as a "CNR school." He suggested that CNR employees, particularly the Blue River operator, had shaped their testimony to protect their jobs. He noted that snow on the telephone lines might have interfered with communications between despatcher Tisdale and Atherton at Red Pass. He concluded by declaring that a conviction could be registered only if Atherton had acted in a way bordering upon deliberate negligence. On May 12 the jury returned a verdict of "not guilty" after brief deliberations.

The Canoe River wreck was less rembered in history than the trial which followed it. John Diefenbaker's colourful defence of A.J. Atherton confirmed the Prairie lawyer's growing reputation as a brilliant legal tactician and an advocate for ordinary Canadians opposed by large (if undefined) interests. It won him sympathy among labour unions, notably the Railroad Brotherhoods, which would help him in the 1957 and 1958 elections. Canoe River would figure prominently in his memoirs (*One Canada: The Crusading Years, 1895-1956*, published in 1975) as well as in books critical of his career (Peter Newman's 1964 classic *Renegade in Power*). For John Diefenbaker, Canoe River was a way station on his passage to the office of prime minister.*

HINTON, Alberta

FEBRUARY 8, 1986

Railway accidents did not cease with the Canoe River disaster, but no tragedy on a comparable scale shook the Canadian scene for more than 35 years. The most spectacular railway accident – a 1981 freight derailment, explosion and fire in Mississauga, Ontario – involved mass community evacuations and a subsequent federal inquiry, but was without loss of life. In the meantime, transportation patterns changed radically. Aircraft replaced trains as the principal means of long-range travel; the two major rail companies reduced their passenger services, then transferred what was left to a Crown corporation, Via Rail, which operated in high-density corridors (chiefly the Montreal-Toronto route), leaving most short- and medium-range intercity travel to buses and private motor cars. Only in the realm of suburban commuter rail services (most notably in the subsidized GO Transit system servicing Toronto) did rail travel show any growth.

Technology changed as well. Diesel locomotives replaced steam; automatic block systems became universal wherever passenger trains ran. Ever more sophisticated safety devices were introduced. In 1950-51 the use of radios had been discussed for communications among train crewmen as well as between crews and despatchers; by 1986 such radios were standard equipment throughout North America.

* Department of Tranport file 3202-10, "Accidents – Collisions and Derailments – Canoe River, British Columbia" found in the National Archives of Canada (Record Group 12, Volume 610) contains the report of the Board of Transport Commissioners as well as clippings on this accident and the subsequent trial.

Computer systems enabled yard personnel to trace the location of trains and even of individual items of rolling stock.

The near-disappearance of major rail tragedies was due as much to the decline in passenger miles travelled as to the new technology. Nevertheless, people still moved by rail, on systems that ultimately were run by fallible humans. Statistically, the likelihood of a serious rail disaster had been cut drastically; it had not been eliminated. Early in 1986, the remotely possible happened. Everything mechanical functioned perfectly; the key humans did not.

The line running from Jasper through Edson to Edmonton was Canadian National Railway track which was also available to Via Rail. Slightly more than half of the 100-mile (160-kilometre) Jasper-Edson stretch was double-tracked. An 11.2-mile (18-kilometre) portion of double track lay between Dalehurst siding on the west and Hargwen siding on the east.

On the morning of February 8, 1986, Via Rail's No. 4 train was eastbound from Jasper to Edmonton. It was made up in unusual fashion because it was actually two trains – one originating in Van-

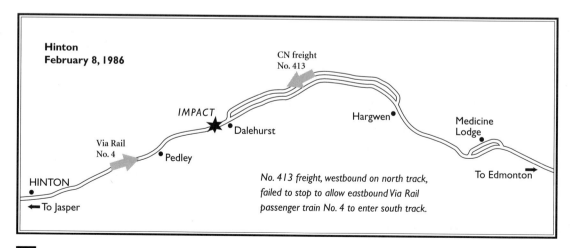

Hinton
February 8, 1986

CN freight
No. 413

IMPACT

Dalehurst

Hargwen

Medicine
Lodge

Via Rail
No. 4

Pedley

HINTON

To Jasper

To Edmonton

No. 413 freight, westbound on north track, failed to stop to allow eastbound Via Rail passenger train No. 4 to enter south track.

couver, the other in Prince Rupert, British Columbia. Thus, the No. 4 consisted of 14 units – two diesel locomotives, followed by a baggage car, day coach with snack bar, dome car with lounge, two sleeping cars, an inoperative locomotive, steam generator car, another baggage car, day/night coach, cafe/lounge car, another sleeper and a further steam generator car. The last item had been added in Jasper for movement to Edmonton, where it was to be serviced.

The No. 4 stopped at Hinton* at 8:20 a.m. and departed that town five minutes later. From there to Dalehurst it was running on single track. Aboard were 94 passengers, 14 passenger service personnel and seven crewmen – a total of 115 people.

The CNR's train No. 413 westbound was a giant collection of rolling stock pulled by three powerful locomotives followed by a high-speed spreader (a piece of track maintenance equipment, used to scatter sand or gravel along the roadbed). Items 5 to 39 were grain-filled hopper cars. These were followed by 7 loaded flatcars, 45 open hopper cars filled with sulphur, 12 tank cars with caustic soda, 8 more with toxic liquids, 6 further grain cars, and a caboose – 118 units, 12,804 tons, 6,124 feet (1,866 metres) long. The crew consisted of John Edward (Jack) Hudson, aged 48 (engineer), Mark Edwards, aged 25 (front-end brakeman) and Wayne Smith, aged 33 (conductor). Hudson and Edwards were riding in the front locomotive; Smith was in the caboose.

Train No. 413 left Edson at 6:40 a.m. The crew took their train into Medicine Lodge siding (a tight fit, as the train was almost as long as the siding itself). After the passage of two eastbound trains, the westbound freight resumed its trip. It departed Medicine Lodge at 8:02 a.m. and reached Hargwen at 8:20 a.m. From that point onwards it was running on the north branch of double track.

At 8:29 a.m. a remote despatcher set the Dalehurst switch to allow

*Although this wreck occurred at Dalehurst siding, 11 miles (17.7 kilometres) east of Hinton, Alberta, contemporary accounts identified it as the "Hinton train collision" and it is so named in this narrative.

Via Rail No. 4 to take the south branch of the upcoming double track. The Via Rail train thus faced signals that were either green (proceed) or yellow over green (slow down for switch). The passenger train approached the switch at 49 miles per hour (78 km/hr), the recommended speed for that section.

Meanwhile, with the switch set, the freight encountered signals that were aimed at slowing and stopping it. A two-light "approach" signal, 13,600 feet (4,145 metres) east of the Dalehurst switch, showed yellow over red (slow down – be prepared to stop). Train No. 413, running at 59 miles per hour (96 km/hr), was already exceeding the road limit by 9 miles an hour (14.5 km/h). It rumbled past the signal and did not slacken speed.

A three-light signal, 490 feet (149 metres) east of the switch, showed red lamps – an order to stop. The weather was clear, the daylight full, and the signal visible for at least 2,900 feet (884 metres). In spite of this, train No. 413 thundered ahead; there was no application of brakes. In violation of all signals, the freight carried on, jumped the switch and continued along what was now single track.

Computer devices installed along the line permitted investigators to reconstruct events with rare precision. Once the freight trespassed upon the single line of rails, the Via Rail No. 4 train was facing a red signal. That was useless at this point. Slight curves on the line obstructed the view of both crews. When the two trains came within sight of each other, there were only 19 seconds left before the collision. The freight's engineer still did not apply brakes. Incredibly, neither did the crew of the Via Rail train. Its crew was either inattentive or frozen with fear.

The time was 8:40.52 a.m. (precise to the second) and the place was 1,270 feet (387 metres) west of the Dalehurst switch. Two or three passengers, from dome car vantage points, realized what was coming and shouted futile warnings. The contest was utterly unequal. The massive freight bowled through the forward part of the passenger train like a hammer through plaster.

A Commission of Inquiry investigated the crash. Mr. Justice René P. Foisy, Alberta Court of Queen's Bench, held 56 days of public hearings and received evidence from 150 parties. His report described the crash in measured phrases:

A burning Via Rail coach at Hinton, 1986. (National Archives of Canada 523648)

The devastation caused by the impact defies description. It is not possible to appreciate the horror that the victims of the collision experienced.

23 persons lost their lives. These included the head-end crews of both trains, 18 occupants of the day coach which was in position 4 on the train and one occupant of the dome car which was in position 5.

The destruction and horror caused by the impact was intensified by fire fuelled by the spilled locomotive diesel oil. The fire broke out almost immediately following the impact and engulfed the lead units of both trains, the baggage car, and the day coach. The contents of a grain car which was thrown into the wreckage also spilled into the day coach. This may possibly have saved some passengers' lives by smothering the fire.

An overall view of the scene of the Hinton disaster shows a jumbled mass of wrecked rolling stock. (National Archives of Canada 523644)

Miraculously, 18 occupants of the day coach managed to escape. Some did so despite having suffered serious injuries.

The passengers in the observation dome escaped through a broken window. The passengers on the lower level of that car escaped through a hole in the side of the car created when one of the cars of the freight train which had been thrown in the air, smashed into the rear of the dome car.

The two sleeper cars immediately following the dome car … were derailed and thrown onto their sides. Some of the passengers in these cars had difficulty finding a route of escape but eventually they did.

The diesel unit, steam generator unit and baggage car in positions 8, 9 and 10 of the train were derailed and overturned – the baggage car only partially. The three passenger cars at the rear of the train, units 11, 12 and 13, did not derail. The occupants of these cars were violently thrown about by the impact and some suffered injury.

The Commission heard accounts of remarkable heroism exhibited by passengers and VIA personnel. The number of survivors, an amazing high number given the extent of the damage to the train equipment, indicates that there must have been many heroic acts performed that were not brought to the Commission's attention.

… On train No. 413 the three diesel locomotives, the high speed spreader, 35 grain hopper cars, seven flatcars carrying large pipes and 33 hopper cars carrying sulphur were destroyed or damaged.

The cost to the two railways, CN and VIA, has been estimated to be in the area of $35,000,000. …*

For many reasons the investigation was a harrowing experience. The inquiry report, published on January 22, 1987, was a disturbing

* Commission of Inquiry: Hinton Train Collision. Report of the Commissioner, The Honourable Mr. Justice René P. Foisy, December 1986. Canadian Government Publishing Centre, Supply and Services Canada.

document, for it probed the very psyche of what Mr. Justice Foisy described as the "railroader culture," which included a general disregard for safety permeating both labour and management within the CNR. In a summary of his report he wrote:

Another view, showing a dome car near the point of impact. (National Archives of Canada 523649)

> This disregard for safety is a reflection of the railroader culture. Within this culture, great value is placed upon loyalty, on endurance, and on productivity. An employee gains standing by being willing to work very long hours regardless of fatigue; he would

An aerial view showing wreckage at Canada's worst recent rail disaster. (National Archives of Canada 523645)

lose standing by claiming a rest period. He gains standing by "protecting" a fellow employee by failing to report rules violations or health or other problems that could adversely affect performance; he would lose standing by drawing such elements to the attention of management and demanding help or support for his co-worker.

This statement leaned heavily upon the "labour" side, but management was also criticised. Mr. Justice Foisy heard officials and supervisors proclaim their respect for safety, yet he also heard evidence that "long standing rule violations occurred routinely without management intervention" – violations they claimed had been hidden from them.

An example of this casual approach to safety was the manner in which the freight crew had boarded their train. Another crew had brought No. 413 from Edmonton to Edson, where engineer Hudson, trainman Edwards and conductor Smith had jumped aboard the freight as it moved slowly through the yards; the old crew had then jumped off. This method, known as changing crews "on the fly," saved time, effort and fuel that would have been expended had the heavy train been halted, then started up again. Managers claimed ignorance of the practice, even though it was common. Changing crews "on the fly" was a flagrant violation of standing operating and safety rules – rules that supervisors and crewmen had tacitly and mutually decided to ignore.

Workers probe the wreckage at the point of impact. (National Archives of Canada 523646)

Another instance of cavalier attitudes to safety involved a device known as the "deadman's pedal." An engineer had to keep the pedal depressed at all times. If he fell asleep or had a heart attack, his foot would slip off the pedal and a cab whistle would sound. If no action followed, automatic braking would occur. However, many engineers found it tiring to keep their foot on the pedal and found ways to by-pass it, usually by placing a heavy weight on it. The locomotive of train No. 413 was so badly crushed and burnt that investigators could not determine whether or not engineer Hudson had bypassed the pedal that morning.

A more advanced safety device, the Reset Safety Control (RSC), was also aimed at ensuring constant crew alertness. It was an electronic system which required crewmen to take some action – even as simple as pushing a button – at regular intervals (between 20 and 127 seconds). If inattentive crews failed to do the necessary task, an alarm would sound, and if that did not rouse the attention of the crew, the brakes would be applied automatically. Neither the freight nor the Via Rail crew had been working in a cab with RSC devices. However, the *second* engine in No. 413's makeup had been equipped with RSC, but it had not been assigned to the head of the freight because it lacked a "comfort cab." Management and union practice was to place locomotives with the more comfortable quarters at the head of freights, even if they had less sophisticated safety equipment than other locomotives in the same train. Even so, a "comfort cab" remained a hot, noisy workplace where boring, repetitive tasks were conducted.

Few remains were found of engineer Hudson and trainman Edwards, but enough was available for medical experts to say that drugs or alcohol were not present in either man's system on February 8, 1986. All the same, the presence of Hudson in the freight locomotive that day represented another "systems failure" and yet another aspect of "railroad culture." Although Hudson was described by his peers as being a "top notch engineer," the weight of evidence pointed to another conclusion. At age 48, he was a medical disaster, suffering from alcoholism, diabetes and high blood pressure, all of which was known to his superiors. He had only recently returned to duty following abdominal surgery.

In the previous nine years Hudson had accumulated 50 demerit points for four previous violations of company and running rules including three instances where equipment was damaged. He might have been awarded more demerit points for other violations (including speeding in a restricted area), but management seemed reluctant to discipline him further. Ten more demerit points would have meant dismissal, and nobody wanted to be responsible for sacking the man. CN's whole programme (or, more accurately, non-programme) of monitoring employee health and enforcing operating discipline was roundly criticised by the Foisy Commission, which virtually accused the company of trying to run a "happy ship" at the expense of running a safe one.

All of these findings described a system where safety was subordinated to other factors. They still did not explain why train No. 413 had run past two sets of functioning signals, jumped a switch and rammed the Via train. The answer seemed to lie in another aspect of "railroad culture." To understand it, one must remember that although the freight crew had boarded their train at Edson, they lived in Jasper. They also operated in an atmosphere of irregular, even erratic work schedules which often involved long shifts. This contrasted sharply with Via Rail methods, by which crews operated on regular, predictable schedules.

The arduous work patterns apparent in CN freight operations were not the result of harsh management. Rather, they were another manifestation of the "railroad culture." There were few incentives for crewmen to take authorized rest periods. Pay systems and peer pressure encouraged long working hours. The latter point was especially strong at away-from-home terminals, when one or more trainmen might sacrifice sleep in the interests of taking an early train back home, even if they or their comrades needed a break.

All crewmen of the Via Rail train had enjoyed proper rest before leaving Jasper. The same was not true of the freight crew. Engineer Jack Hudson, although rested before leaving Jasper, had caught about $3^1/_2$ hours of sleep in the previous 16 hours; it may have been only $3^1/_2$ hours in the previous 20. Trainman Edwards, who shared the cab with Hudson, had slept less than five hours in the same period. His case was complicated by the fact that he was suffering from flu, although he had not booked out sick. The conductor, Wayne Smith, had taken no more than four hours sleep preceding the fatal run of train No. 413.

There was no certain proof that Hudson and Edwards had both fallen asleep in the cab on the morning of February 8 – only the probability, based on their actions and known rest periods, that they had done so. In these circumstances, one man might still have prevented the disaster – conductor Wayne Smith, far at the rear of the train. His evidence at the Foisy Commission hearings was contradictory; in the end, Mr. Justice Foisy dismissed Smith's testimony as being unreliable.

Railroad practice was that front-end and rear-end crews should be in regular communications, particularly when approaching signals. Thus, as No. 413 arrived at Hargwen, Hudson radioed back to Smith that the signals was green; this radio call was heard by the crew of a following freight. As train No. 413 ran towards the Dalehurst signals, either Hudson or Smith should have called up to confirm the signals there. If such a call could not be made, the conductor would be authorized to pull the brake cord in the caboose and stop the train.

He could do the same thing if he felt the train was going too fast or was out of control.

Smith, who was very nervous and high strung when testifying, declared that at no time did he sense No. 413 to be out of control. Given that he had no speedometer in the caboose, he obviously misjudged the freight's speed, which was excessive for some three miles before the crash. He also testified that he did try to raise Hudson on two radios – a portable grey radio and a red set installed permanently in the caboose – but neither set seemed to be working. In this situation he would have been justified in pulling the brake cord. He did not do so – a second misjudgment.

The conductor's testimony was subjected to harsh cross-examination. Notwithstanding Smith's statements, it was obvious that no other train crew in the area had picked up his radio calls to the front-end crew. Moreover, the radios that supposedly did not function before the crash were working perfectly immediately afterwards; Smith reported the impact to a despatcher within seconds.

Indeed, it was difficult to say exactly where Smith was sitting in the ten minutes leading up to the accident. His proper post would have been in the cupola of the caboose, where he would have had a good view of the train and signals. He stated that after trying to radio the front-end crew and just before the crash he had moved from the cupola to a desk at the rear of the caboose. There was no reason for him to be anywhere other than the cupola during the run from Hargwen to Dalehurst; given that the desk seat was more comfortable than the cupola, the suspicion was that Smith had left his proper station earlier than stated, and that he had been neglecting his duties.

In the end, Mr. Justice Foisy was unable to state precisely *why* train No. 413 had run past two signals and a switch into the path of Via Rail No. 4. Having eliminated equipment failure, drugs, alcohol and signal malfunctions, he drew back from laying blame on any specific individual, preferring to criticise the general "railroader culture" which found little room for safety in rail operations. By implication, any possible negligence by the crewmen of train No. 413 was symptomatic of a broader malaise which made possible even further disasters on Canadian tracks.

EPILOGUE

An overview of Canadian railway disasters will hardly provide one with earth-shaking insights, but an author is entitled to some concluding observations about the subject. Having perused accounts of 30 terrible accidents, the reader may be struck by some of the same impressions that occurred to me.

One is that we, as a species, have made some progress as sentient beings. There is more to this than improved technology. The indifference to foreigners showed in the New Westminster and Brandon wrecks is strange to us. If Canadians still harbour prejudices and meanness, such characteristics are not so pronounced as a century ago.

We have progressed in other ways. Shopping-centre tabloids notwithstanding, the standards of journalism are incomparably better than those of the distant past. The 19th-century press seemed intent on shocking without necessarily informing. The spectacle of rival papers exploiting a tragedy to attack one another is something with which we are unfamiliar.

If one thing stands out, however, it is the swiftness with which investigations were carried out and trials conducted. It is entirely possible that not all truths were ferreted out, nor all culpable parties arraigned in the dock. Nevertheless, in an age when inquiries are prolonged for months, almost beyond public caring, one might look back upon these incidents and marvel at how expeditiously the system worked. Swift justice may have been rough justice, but in the opinion of this writer, its speedy execution, when memories were still fresh, had something to commend it to the modern age of protracted, costly and repeated inquests which have worn down their participants, exhausted public interest, and served chiefly to employ a corpulent legal profession.

Curiously, this leads one to ponder railway accidents in the context of contemporary culture. The Foisy Commission, investigating the 1986 Hinton wreck, identified a macho "railway culture" which sometimes interfered with adherence to safety procedures. It is difficult to discern this "railway culture" in earlier wrecks, but it may have played a role in the Craig's Road collision (1895), in which one engineer was suspected of having drunk beer while on duty. Different forms of institutional cultures are now being recognized, including corporate assumptions that hold back women or promote from within informal cliques. The most notorious Canadian example has been the deviant cultures that infected portions of the Canadian armed forces; disbandment of the Canadian Airborne Regiment, though hotly debated, was clearly an instance of drastic surgery aimed at a cancerous growth. Other cultures may be identified, their hallmark being the gradual separation of groups from the general community, turning inwards with incestuous self-absorbtion to the detriment of group members and the society as a whole.

As one reviews major wrecks, scores of other accidents come to light. A typical example is one that occurred on March 5, 1927. A gasoline speeder (more widely known as a "jigger") collided with a freight train near Otterburn, Manitoba. The two men aboard the vehicle, Henry Vernette, aged 43, and Hjalmar Nystrom, 47, both of Carberry, were killed instantly. The cause of the accident was obvious – slippery tracks and reduced visibility in a snowstorm – and there was no inquest. The accident made the Manitoba papers and later the pages of the *Labour Gazette*, but went unreported elsewhere. Vernette left a wife and children. Nystrom, an Icelandic immigrant, 20 years resident in Manitoba, was survived only by a niece. It was not a disaster in the accepted sense of the word, but nevertheless it teaches a sombre moral.

Disasters bringing tragedy to many highlight inherent dangers, destructive trends and insular occupational cultures. Yet for every major accident there are hundreds of smaller ones. The accident that kills one man is as much a catastrophe for his friends and family as the crash that wipes out dozens. The quantity of suffering may be less; the quality of loss is roughly the same from one individual to the next. It should not take a serial killer or a rampaging psychopath to point up dangers within our society; dozens of isolated incidents of a similar kind should offer similar warnings. However distant the tragedy or seemingly insignificant the carnage, it is well to remember John Donne:

Any man's death diminishes me, because I am involved in Mankind; and therefore never send to know for whom the bell tolls; it tolls for thee.

Index